P9-BJD-961

SPORT CLIMBS
in the Canadian Rockies

John Martin and Jon Jones

Fifth Edition

Rocky
Mountain Books

Front cover: Knut Rokne on Jason Lives (12d/13a), Lake Louise.
Photo Jeff Moore, Avoca Images.
Back cover: Climbers on Cardiac Arete (10d), Grand Sentinel.
Photo Eric Hsiung.

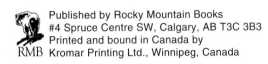

Published by Rocky Mountain Books
#4 Spruce Centre SW, Calgary, AB T3C 3B3
Printed and bound in Canada by
RMB Kromar Printing Ltd., Winnipeg, Canada

Copyright © 1995, 1996, 1998, 2000, 2002 John Martin & Jon Jones

All rights reserved. No part of this book may be reproduced
in any form without permission in writing from the publisher,
except by a reviewer who may quote brief passages in a review.

We acknowledge the financial support of the Government
of Canada through the Book Publishing Industry Develop-
ment Program (BPIDP) for our publishing activities.

Canadian Cataloguing in Publication Data
Martin, John, 1947-
  Sport climbs in the Canadian Rockies

  Includes index.
  ISBN 0-921102-91-7

  1. Rock climbing--Rocky Mountains, Canadian (B.C. and Alta.)--Guide-
books.* 2. Rocky Mountains, Canadian (B.C. and Alta.)--Guidebooks.* I.
Jones, Jon. II. Title.
GV199.44.C22A4565 2002 796.52'23'0971233   C2002-910409-2

I wonder who pays for all these hangers?

TABVAR does.
Support your sport
(see page 8)

JD LeBlanc on Doppio (13b), Carrot Creek (p.129). Photo Jon Jones

TABLE OF CONTENTS

LIST OF MAPS

Scott Milton on Leviathan (14b), Acephale. (p. 53).
Photo Sandra Studer.

What the Guidebook Covers

The guidebook includes all the main sport climbing areas in the Canadian Rockies except those near Jasper (which are covered by a separate guidebook). Most of the routes are fully equipped sport climbs, but some short gear climbs are included as well.

Information on multi-pitch, traditional climbs in the Rockies can be found in *Bow Valley Rock* by Chris Perry and Joe Josephson and *Ghost Rock* by Joe Josephson, Chris Perry and Andy Genereux.

Route Grading

The guidebook uses standard North American grading, minus the "5" prefix. Exception: a few of the routes have "-" and "+" instead of letter grades. "-" equates to a and a/b; "+" to c/d and d. "R" means a potentially dangerous runout and "X" means if you fall you'll deck. Quality ratings are 0 (ok), 1 (good) or 2 (better) stars.

Key to Topo Drawings

The topos are drawn using standard North American conventions, as shown.

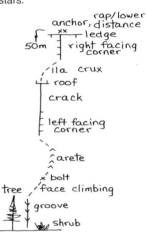

The Rock

Most of the routes are on **limestone,** a soft and often highly fractured rock that gives mainly face climbs. "Clean" protection opportunities are limited and loose holds may occasionally be found even on well-groomed routes. In the Lake Louise area, the climbs are on **quartzite,** a high quality, hard rock with lots of horizontal holds and a fair number of protectable cracks. Routes have also been developed on **siltstone** (Spray Slabs), which is like sandstone minus the texture and the holds, and **conglomerate** (Cowbell Crag), which offers pebble pulling and some crack climbing.

The Weather

The rock climbing season usually starts sometime in April and ends in early October. In warm years it may be possible to climb comfortably as early as February or as late as November. The warmest early and late season areas are Crag X, The Sanctuary, Barrier Mountain, Wasootch Creek, Cowbell Crag, Moose Mountain, White Buddha, and Bataan.

Gear

Rope – 60 m recommended; 2 ropes occasionally needed
Quickdraws – 8-10 for most climbs; up to 16 on longer pitches
Non-fixed gear – as indicated throughout the guide
Helmet – suit yourself, but some cliffs have rockfall hazard
Stick-clipper – recommended—many newer routes are set up for stick-clipping

Camping & Climbers' Lodgings

Bow Valley   provincial campgrounds accessible from Hwy. 1 and Hwy. 1X.
Banff Park   Parks Canada campgrounds at Banff, Castle Mtn. and Lake Louise
Kananaskis   numerous provincial campgrounds
Ghost   unrestricted camping
Canmore   Alpine Club of Canada Clubhouse 403-678-3200
Lake Louise Alpine Centre 403-522-2200

Current information on camping outside the national park is available at the Tourist Information Centre at the west entrance to Canmore.

Parks Canada Offices (Mon-Fri, 08:00-16:00)

• Banff   403-762-1550
• Lake Louise 403-522-3833
• Calgary   403-292-4401

Climbing Gyms

Calgary   Calgary Climbing Centre   403-252-6778   www.calgaryclimbing.com
             The Stronghold   403-276-6484   www.strongholdclimbing.com
Canmore   Vsion Climbing Gym   403-678-8803

Lead That Route

Sport climbs are built for leading, so there is no good reason for messing around at the tops of cliffs to set up topropes. On the contrary, there are excellent reasons not to:
• you may dislodge loose rocks, putting others at risk
• you may contribute to soil erosion and vegetation damage.

   So we ask that you stick to routes that at least one member of your party can lead. Alternatively, go to Wasootch Creek, which is an accepted toproping venue.

Environmental Stewardship

Courtesy – Climbing areas are public places, not your private domain. Please respect the rights of others. Loud swearing and other loutish behaviour may alienate other users.
Litter – Abandoned slings on sport routes constitute litter as well as being a potential safety hazard. If you have to retreat from a route, and you haven't learned how to retrieve your sling after rappelling from it, please use a biner.
Dogs are great, but not at climbing areas. The main dog-related issues are safety, nuisance and sanitation.
Human Feces – Inside the canyons, pack feces out. Outside the canyons, stay at least 15 m from streams and above high water mark; bury feces; burn paper or pack it out.
Save Our Stone – Limestone quickly becomes permanently polished and slippery when punished by the flailing feet of overmatched climbers. Bad footwork is not just bad form—it kills climbs. Please don't set up topropes for greatly overmatched climbers.
Tick Marks – Please erase tick marks after you've finished with a climb so other leaders can enjoy working out the moves for themselves.

New Route Guidelines

The following guidelines and legalities apply to new route creation in the guidebook area:

- The route should be safe for an on-sight lead by a climber competent at its grade.
- Pitons and nylon webbing are not acceptable as permanent fixtures on sport routes.
- Avoid squeezing in routes close to established climbs.
- Creating holds or attaching imported holds is illegal in national and provincial parks and not very popular elsewhere.
- Reinforcement of existing holds with glue and removal of vegetation are illegal in national and provincial parks.
- New route creation is not allowed at King Creek (Peter Lougheed Provincial Park).
- Provincial government approval is now required for the creation of new sport climbing areas on public lands outside the national parks. No approval is needed for new cliffs within established areas. For more details, contact TABVAR (address below).

Who Owns the Climbs?

The climbs in this book are on public property. No group, including an instructional group, has the right to "take over" an area or to discourage other climbers from being there. If you have a rope up a climb, use it or lose it (the climb, that is)!

WHO PAYS FOR ALL THOSE HANGERS?

Developing sport crags is expensive! Hardware costs for a single fully equipped 25 m route are in the $45-50 range. All told, the climbs in this guide represent many tens of thousands of dollars in gear costs.

Since 1993, nearly all the new climbs and retrofitting done within the guidebook area—more than 800 routes in all—have been funded by TABVAR (The Association of Bow Valley Rock Climbers), a registered non-profit organization established to represent the interests of local sport climbers. TABVAR's mandate includes:

- securing and disbursing funds for hardware on new routes
- organizing and funding the retrofitting of older routes to sport standards
- environmental and access matters.

You can help. Send a donation to TABVAR, 79 Rosery Drive NW, Calgary, AB, T2K 1L4.

TABVAR's main benefactor has been Mountain Equipment Co-op, which has donated over $13,000 to date. The climbing community owes them a huge "thank you." TABVAR is greatly indebted to The Stronghold Inc. for donations of cash, time and the use of their facilities for fund-raisers and for storing guidebook updates on their website and also to Deb Bisztriczky for maintaining the update web pages. TABVAR would also like to thank Dave Bakelaar, Eric Dumerac and Keith Haberl for their help with fund raising; Eric Dumerac, Manley Feineberg II, Rob Owens, Chic Scott, Raphael Slawinski and Dave Thomson for donating the proceeds of their slide shows to TABVAR; and all those climbers who have made donations to TABVAR.

Thank you: Anonymous (Calgary), Anonymous (Cochrane), Martin Armitage, Wes Armitage, Di Batten & Doug Bruce, Michael Baxter, Simon Berry, Barry Blanchard, Michael Bradley, Janet Brygger, Ronald Cattaruzza, Ken Charlton, Roger Chayer, Dwayne Congdon, Dave & Carolyn Cousins, Brenda Critchley, David Dornian, Geoff Fraser, Sandee Greatrex,

Jiri Havelka, Jo Kent, Karl Klassen & Mary Clayton, Sean Lunny, Craig McLurg, Jeff Nazarchuk, Michael O'Hagan, J.C. Penner, Jacquie Puscus, Mike Radik, Leslie Reid, Bill Rennie, David Robinson, Gunter Sammet, Marg Saul, Mark Shalom, Dean Skoubis & Cindy Grand, Douglas Smith, Jeff Taylor & Julie Hart, D. Thesen, Dean Tremaine, Angus Watson, Tony & Sarah Whitehouse, Kelly Wilson and Scott Woodcock for your generous donations.

Special thanks go to Brian Bailey, Brian Balazs, Ilona Berbekar, Climbers Anonymous, Devonian Properties Inc., Paul Gray & Robin Reid, Bonnie Hamilton & Jamie McVicar, Robyn Lawrick & Bob Shaw, Pam Pearson, Brett Mitchelson & Anne Horsley, Carey Robillard, Nancy Robillard, David, Jordan & Sue Slaght, Steve Stahl, Andy Skuce, Sharon Wood and John Woodcock, for very generous donations of $200 or more.

Extra special thanks go to Brent Allardyce, Dave Carley, Bonnie Hamilton & Jamie McVicar, Ken MacDonald, Matt Lunny & Fiona Pinnell, Rob McNeil and Andrea Petzold for their extremely generous donations of $500 or more.

TABVAR also gratefully acknowledges donations from the following organizations and clubs: Adventure Dynamics Inc., The Alpine Club of Canada, The Alpine Club of Canada (Calgary section), The Alpine Club of Canada (Saskatchewan section), The Calgary Mountain Club, Rocky Mountain Books, U. of C. Campus Rec., YAK Alpine Guides, Yamnuska Inc.

New Route Information

Comments, corrections and new route information can be sent to the authors c/o Rocky Mountain Books, #4 Spruce Centre SW, Calgary, AB T3C 3B3. Or e-mail us at jones@geo.ucalgary.ca.

Updated route information will be posted on TABVAR's link on The Stronghold home page **www.strongholdclimbing.com**.

Acknowledgements

Thanks to: Richard Akitt, Peter Arbic, Brian Bailey, Roger Chayer, Greg Cornell, Dave Dornian, Eric Dumerac, Ben Firth, Greg Golovach, Keith Haberl, Lynda Howard, Bruce Howatt, Shaun King, Karl Krause, JD LeBlanc, Kelly MacLeod, Jamie McVicar, Chris Miller, Pat Morrow, Marcus Norman, Chris Perry, Dave Thomson, Murray Toft, Daren Tremaine, Mark Whalen, Scott Withers, Brian Wyvill, Colin Zacharias and Rocky Mountain Books.

Special thanks to Andy Genereux for his continued, invaluable contribution.

Check Conditions Using the Web

Webcams

Sunshine Village: www.skibanff.com/Sun99/index.asp
Sulphur Mountain (Banff): www.worldweb.com/ParksCanada-Banff/weather.html
Lake Louise: web.alberta.com/alberta/skycams/louise.htm

Weather conditions and forecasts

Environment Canada Banff, Canmore & Kananaskis (Bow Valley): weatheroffice.ec.gc.ca
CNN for Banff, Canmore, Lake Louise: www. weather.com

Trail Conditions and Closures

www.discoveralberta.com/ParksCanada-Banff/trailreport.html
1-800-748-7275 toll-free from anywhere in North America

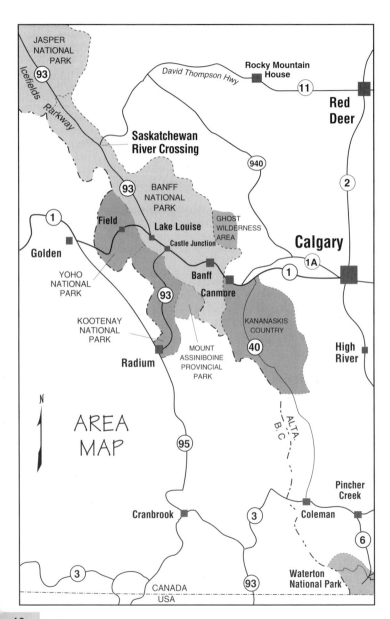

JASPER
NATIONAL
PARK

Icefields Parkway

(93)

David Thompson Hwy

Rocky Mountain
House

(11)

Red
Deer

(2)

Saskatchewan
River Crossing

(940)

(93)

BANFF
NATIONAL
PARK

(1)

Field

Lake Louise

GHOST
WILDERNESS
AREA

Calgary

Golden

Castle Junction

(1A)

YOHO
NATIONAL
PARK

Banff

(1)

(93)

Canmore

KOOTENAY
NATIONAL
PARK

KANANASKIS
COUNTRY

(40)

High
River

Radium

MOUNT
ASSINIBOINE
PROVINCIAL
PARK

N

AREA
MAP

(95)

ALTA.
B.C.

Pincher
Creek

(3)

Cranbrook

Coleman

(6)

(3)

CANADA
USA

(93)

Waterton
National Park

INDEX OF MAIN CLIMBING AREAS

Area	Page No.	Number of routes at each grade								Total
		2–6	7–8	9	10	11	12	13	14	
Acéphale	46				3	7	23	13	3	49
Barrier	270	5	12	12	32	28	10			99
Bataan	168				11	25	18	3		57
Burstall Slabs	310		2	2	9	8				21
Carrot Creek	113			1	32	62	22	5		122
Coral Crag	107		2	1	12	15				30
Cougar Canyon	144	1	7	22	107	47	3			187
Cowbell Crag	304	6	7	7	16					36
Crag X	182			1	4	5	1			11
Ghost	235	3	20	13	55	42	10			143
Grassi Lakes	75	4	4	6	33	18	22			87
Grotto Canyon	185	14	25	26	85	53	19	5		227
Heart Creek	56	7	12	16	67	18	8	5		133
Kanga/EEOR	89	1	4	1	13	13	2			34
Kid/Nanny Goat	219		1	6	26	2				35
Lake Louise	12	19	19	26	65	46	26	2		203
McDougall Slabs	297	1	5	7	16	1				30
Moose Mountain	316			1	11	35	9			56
Paradise Wall	42				10	4				14
Porcupine Creek	281		5	4	12	2				23
Prairie Creek	326		1	4	7	11	16	5		44
Raven Crag	98				1	1	5	3		10
Sanctuary	216				5	8	4			17
Spray Slabs	99				11	5				16
Steve Canyon	214	2	2	2	15	3				24
Stoneworks	136			4	18	15	5			42
Tunnel Mountain	100			2	7	2				11
Wasootch Slabs	284	28	32	14	23	7				104
White Buddha	332	1		1	9	2	2			15

THE BACK OF THE LAKE (Lake Louise)

Situated in the middle of one of the most famous mountain views in the world—Lake Louise and Mount Victoria as seen from Chateau Lake Louise—the Back of the Lake offers spectacular climbing on steep, clean quartzite faces, cracks, and arêtes. This is a mixed trad/sport climbing area and both styles of climbs are included here to provide complete coverage. High elevation and cold air drainage from glaciers make for a relatively short climbing season at Lake Louise, lasting most years from early June to late August. Most of the cliffs in the Main Area face south or east and get plenty of sun. Wait for warm, dry weather to climb at The Other Side (of the lake) though—the cliffs face north, see little sun and being lichen-covered, are *extremely* slick when wet. By September the sun struggles to clear the high peaks that encircle the lake and cooler air and lengthening shadows usually limit climbing to the more southerly facing crags; but even here it may be too cold for comfort until the afternoon.

Quick Start:

If, just after you left the parking lot, you passed a big hotel on the right with a guy wearing leather shorts out front who was trying to play "Amazing Grace" on an alpenhorn and if you are presently standing in horseshit in front of the first cliff you came to, you are at the Trailside area. Turn to page 39. To find the topo for the next crag to your left (facing the rock) turn back a page. Repeat as necessary.

Approach

From Highway 1, follow road signs (and likely, a long line of RV's, campers and tour buses) to Lake Louise. There is usually a Parks Canada checkpoint at the entrance to the parking lot where you can pay the Banff National Park entrance fee, if you have not already done so. At the height of the tourist season, finding a parking space can be difficult during the middle part of the day, so plan to arrive early.

The Main Area: Follow the tourist trail past the Chateau and along the northeast shore of the lake. After about 30 minutes the trail ascends a short hill ("Heart Attack Hill") and arrives at the Trailside area, close to the start of *Aeroflot* (see p. 39).

The Other Side: The crags here may be reached either via The Main Area or directly from the parking lot. Goblin Wall and Rockfall Wall are best approached directly from the parking lot (see p. 14, 16) whereas Fraggle Rock, Hydrotherapy Wall and Kaleidoscope Pinnacle are best accessed via The Main Area, by fording the icy waters of the outlet stream of Victoria Glacier.

MAIN AREA OVERVIEW

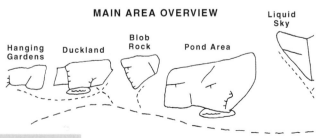

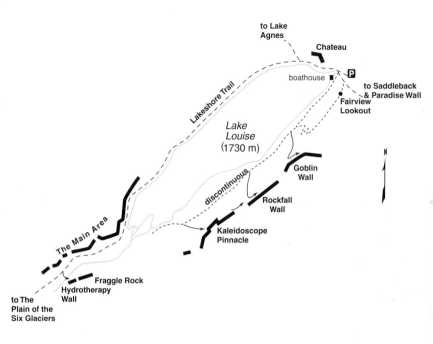

to Lake Agnes

Chateau

boathouse

P

to Saddleback & Paradise Wall

Fairview Lookout

Lakeshore Trail

Lake Louise
(1730 m)

Goblin Wall

discontinuous

Rockfall Wall

Kaleidoscope Pinnacle

The Main Area

Fraggle Rock

Hydrotherapy Wall

to The Plain of the Six Glaciers

N

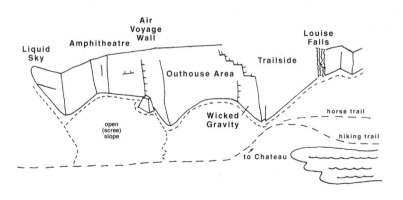

Liquid Sky

Amphitheatre

Air Voyage Wall

Outhouse Area

Trailside

Louise Falls

open (scree) slope

Wicked Gravity

horse trail

hiking trail

to Chateau

GOBLIN WALL

This is a cool place to climb in every sense of the word. There are some great multi-pitch climbs here in a spectacular setting high above the lake and away from the crowds. Wear a helmet, as there is occasional rockfall from the slopes above the wall.

Approach

Locate an unsigned trail that starts just above the boathouse at the end of the lake and runs along the southeast shore. Follow this to where it climbs steeply and switchbacks to the left (about 10 minutes). From the apex of this bend, go straight ahead (through a few trees) to a rough trail that crosses a talus slope. (This trail continues the length of the southeast side of the lake, but has fallen into disrepair and is difficult to follow in a few places.) Follow this trail a short distance and then climb up steeply on large blocks, skirting below lobes of slide alder, until it is possible to head directly towards Goblin Wall. Turn a small cliff band on its right and gain the grassy terrace that runs along the foot of the face (40 minutes from parking). Note: You can cut over to Rockfall Wall from here but this is **not** recommended; the slope is steep, the footing is poor and the rockfall hazard is high.

Descent

You will need 2 ropes to descend most of the climbs here. The easiest descent from the *Goblin Arête* is to rap to stance 2 of *Love at First Sight* (about 30 m). From here it is 60 m directly to the ground, or one can rap 30 m to stance 1 of *Love at First Sight* and thence to the ground (35 m).

GOBLIN WALL

A	Ammonia Whore**	10c	gear to 5"
B	A Sensitive Boy**	10c	gear to 3"
C	Goblin Arête**	11b/c	gear to 2.5", TCUs, RPs
D	Love at First Sight**	11b	gear to 2.5", TCUs, RPs, dbl M Rocks
E	project		
F	project		
G	Ghostbusters*	10a	gear to 3"
H	(Yet Another) Mr Natural**	10c	gear to 3.5"
I	Frigid Hoar*	10a	gear to 3"
J	Seeds of Dissent*	11a	gear to 2", pins
K	Arctic Power	9	gear

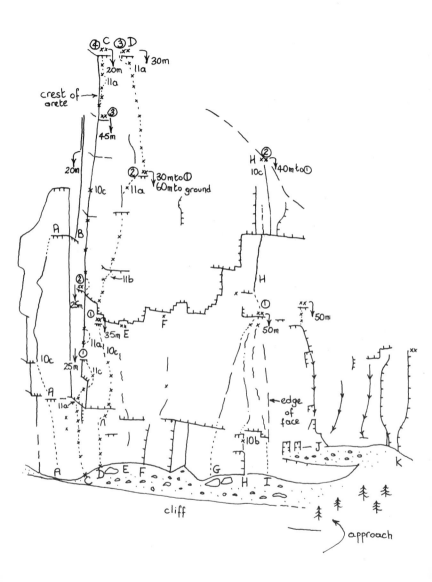

④ C ③ D

xx xx ↓ 30m

20m

11a

11a

crest of → arete

xx ③

45m

20m

10c

11a

② xx

A   B

30m to ①
60m to ground

H xx ②

10c

40m to ①

② xx ── 11b

25m

①

35m E

F

H

① xx

50m

11a 10c

① xx

25m

11c

10c

A

11a

edge of face

10b

J xx xx

A

C D E F

G

H I

K

50m

cliff

approach

ROCKFALL WALL

As the name suggests, there *is* rockfall danger here, so **wear a helmet**. However, falling rocks usually land away from the cliff face and you should be safe when you are close to it. Most rock fall occurs during spring when the snow melts, during heavy rain, or when it is very windy. Occasionally, goats or lost tourists dislodge loose rocks from high on Fairview Mountain.

Approach

Start as for Goblin Wall (above) but continue on the trail that runs along the southeast side of the lake until you are directly below Rockfall Wall—a very clean looking section of greenish-grey rock, about 50 m right of the apex of the prominent scree cone. Scramble up the right edge of an area of large boulders to a rough trail that runs along the base of the rock face (45 - 50 minutes from parking).

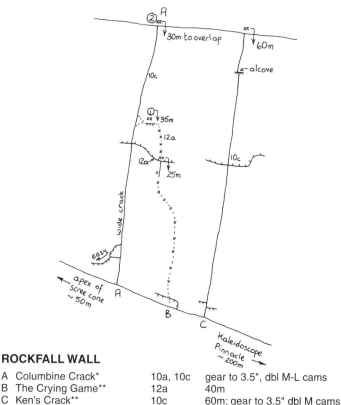

ROCKFALL WALL

A	Columbine Crack*	10a, 10c	gear to 3.5", dbl M-L cams
B	The Crying Game**	12a	40m
C	Ken's Crack**	10c	60m; gear to 3.5" dbl M cams

KALEIDOSCOPE PINNACLE

Approach

The best approach to Kaleidoscope Pinnacle is via The Main Area. Cross to the far side of the outwash flats opposite the Pond Area, fording several distributaries on the way, to a boulder field at the end of the lake. Follow the trail along the south shore of the lake for about 5 minutes to a clearing in thick bushes. A steep, climbers' trail branches right from here and leads up, through bushes at first, to Kaleidoscope Pinnacle (about 20 minutes from the main area). Rockfall Wall can be reached from here by continuing to the left (N.E.) for 5 minutes or so on a rough path that runs along the base of Kaleidoscope Pinnacle.

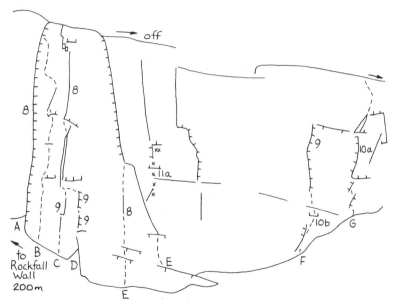

KALEIDOSCOPE PINNACLE

A	Kaleidoscope Left	8	120m; gear to 4"
B	Santa's Revenge*	10a	120 m; gear to 3"
C	Lake View Crescent	9	120 m; gear to 4"
D	Nautilus**	9	120 m; gear to 4"
E	Kaleidoscope Right*	7 or 8	120 m; gear to 4"
F	Cornflakes	10b	70 m; gear to 3"
G	Tears of a Clown*	10a	70 m; gear to 3"

FRAGGLE ROCK AND HYDROTHERAPY WALL

Fraggle Rock is the dark, lichen-covered buttress directly opposite Blob Rock. To its right is a broken, treed area and then a nice looking buttress with a very distinctive, broad white stripe on its left end; this is Hydrotherapy Wall.

Approach

Follow a small but prominent path that starts beside the main trail near Duckland and crosses the river flats to the main stream channel and Hydrotherapy Wall. Unfortunately, this crag endures perpetual shade and is the coldest in the area; the rock is seldom warm and, most years, the gully to its left retains ice until summer's end!

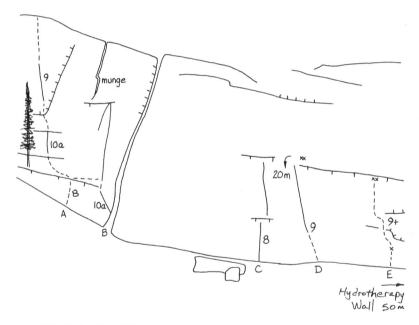

FRAGGLE ROCK

A	For Your Eyes Only	10a	gear to 3"
B	Fandango	10a	gear to 3"
C	Frick*	8	gear to 2" no anchors
D	Frack**	9	gear to 2"
E	Fricken-Fracken	9/10a	gear to 2"

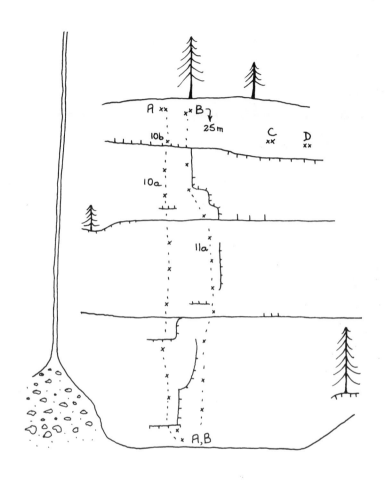

HYDROTHERAPY WALL

A Troubled Waters*   10b/c
B Grin and Bear It**   11a/b
C project
D project

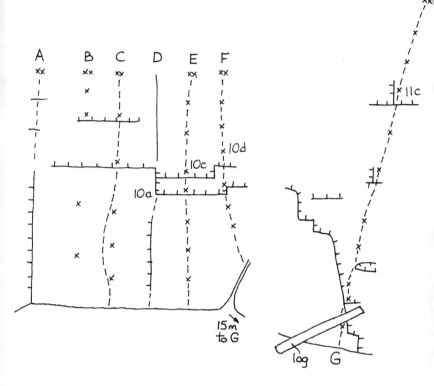

HANGING GARDENS

A	Cornerstone	9	gear
B	project		
C	Flying Squirrel	12a	
D	Green Invasion**	10a	gear to 2.5"
E	No More Tangles**	10c	
F	Three on a Tree**	10d	
G	Casa Yo' Mama	11c	

*Corrie Robb on Heart of Darkness P1
(10b), Lake Louise (p. 40).
Photo Roger Chayer/TALUS Photographics.*

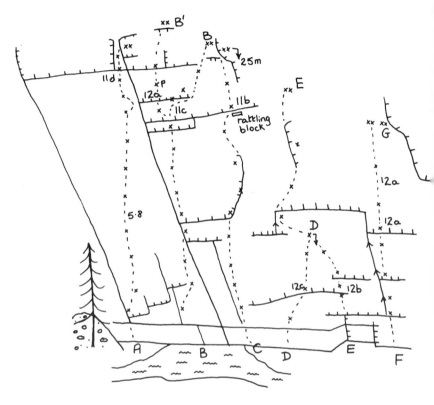

DUCKLAND, FRONT

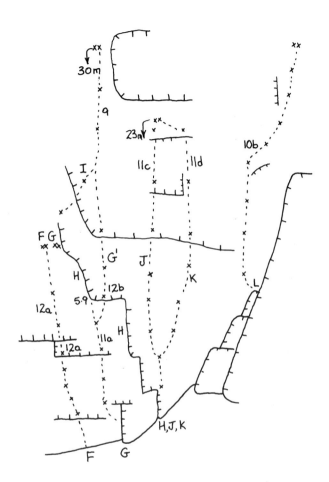

DUCKLAND, RIGHT

G	Howard the Duck**	11a	
G'	Howard the Duck (ext.)	12b	
H	Off the Air**	9	gear to 2.5"
I	On the Air*	9	
J	Wild Frontiers**	11c/d	
K	Cowgirls in the Rain**	11d/12a	
L	Age of Electric*	10b/c	

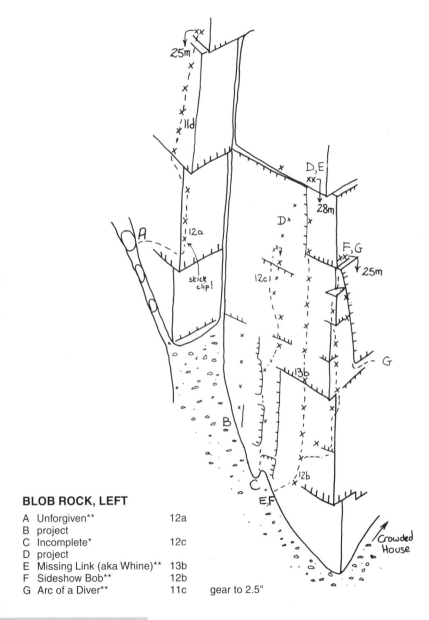

BLOB ROCK, LEFT

A	Unforgiven**	12a
B	project	
C	Incomplete*	12c
D	project	
E	Missing Link (aka Whine)**	13b
F	Sideshow Bob**	12b
G	Arc of a Diver**	11c	gear to 2.5"

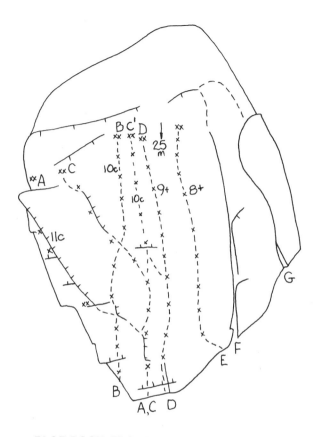

BLOB ROCK, FRONT

A	Arc of a Diver**	11c	gear to 2.5"
B	Crowded House**	10c	
C	If in Doubt*	9	
C'	Latest Squeeze**	10c/d	
D	The Black Knight**	9/10a	
E	Castle Anthrax**	8+	
F	5.4 Dick	4	gear to 4"
G	Scary Business	4	gear to 3"

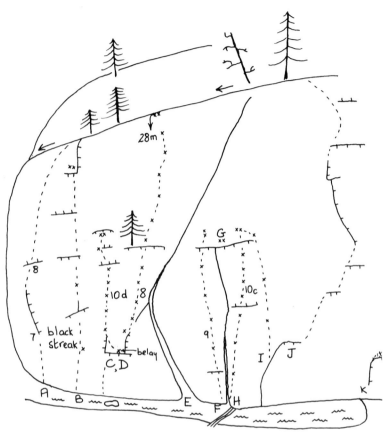

POND AREA, LEFT

A	Schlomo's Nose Job	8	gear to 3"
B	Delirious	9	gear to 3"
C	Headbanger*	10d	
D	10-69*	8	
E	Golden Gully	3	not recommended
F	Way Drilled*	9	
G	Way Frizzled	4	gear
H	The Web**	10c	
I	NFG	10c	
J	Wandering Jew	7	gear to 3"

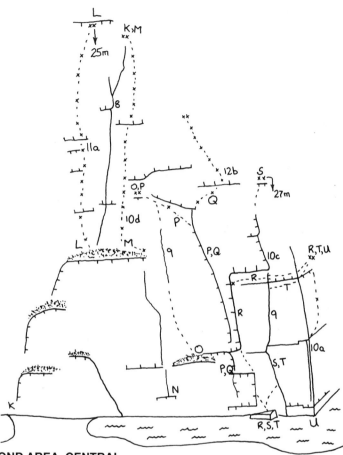

POND AREA, CENTRAL

K	Genius	8	gear to 3.5"
L	Original Sin**	11a	
M	Forbidden Fruit**	10d	
N	The Land God Gave to Cain	8	gear to 2.5"
O	A Life of Crime	9	gear to 3"
P	Good Bye Mr Spalding*	9	gear to 3"
Q	Filigree and Shadow*	12b	
R	Swift Flyte	10a	gear to 3"
S	Vital Transfiguration**	10c	gear to 4"
T	Swamp Thing*	9	gear to 3"
U	Splash Down*	10a	wired nuts, TCUs

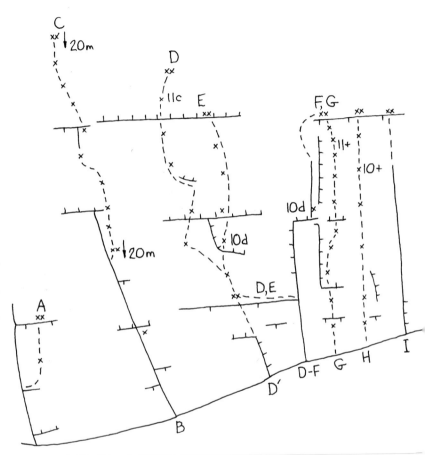

POND AREA, RIGHT

A	Splash Down*	10a	nuts, TCUs
B	Stubborn Nut	8	gear to 2.5"
C	Genetically Challenged**	10d	
D	Kobiyashi Mahru**	11c	
D'	alt. start	10a	
E	Vulcan Princess*	10d	
F	Just Jazzed P1**	10d	gear to 3"
G	Eastern Block**	11d	
H	Route 36**	10c/d	
I	Russian Roulette	8	gear

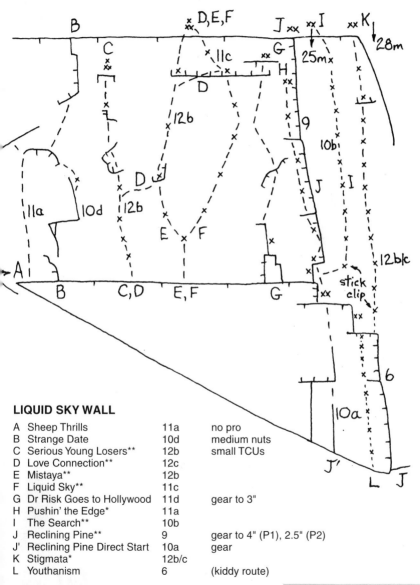

LIQUID SKY WALL

A	Sheep Thrills	11a	no pro
B	Strange Date	10d	medium nuts
C	Serious Young Losers**	12b	small TCUs
D	Love Connection**	12c	
E	Mistaya**	12b	
F	Liquid Sky**	11c	
G	Dr Risk Goes to Hollywood	11d	gear to 3"
H	Pushin' the Edge*	11a	
I	The Search**	10b	
J	Reclining Pine**	9	gear to 4" (P1), 2.5" (P2)
J'	Reclining Pine Direct Start	10a	gear
K	Stigmata*	12b/c	
L	Youthanism	6	(kiddy route)

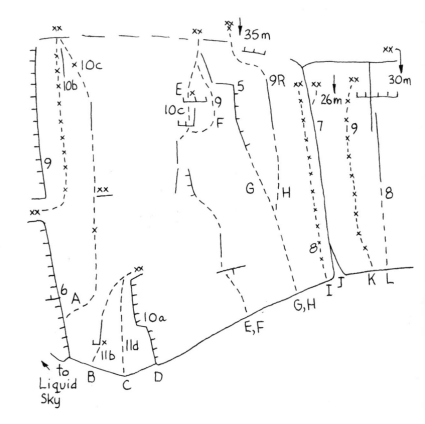

THE AMPHITHEATRE, LEFT

A	The Prowler	10c	gear to 3"
B	Maniac Cure	11b	RPs
C	Donkey Show	11d	toprope
D	Manicure Crack*	10a	gear to 3.5"
E	Misled Youth*	10c	gear to 3"
F	Blade Runner*	9	gear to 3"
G	Mountain Greenery*	5	gear to 4"
H	Rainbow Connection	9	gear to 2.5"
I	FNG*	8	
J	Propeller	7	TCUs and 5 QDs
K	Imaginary Face**	9	

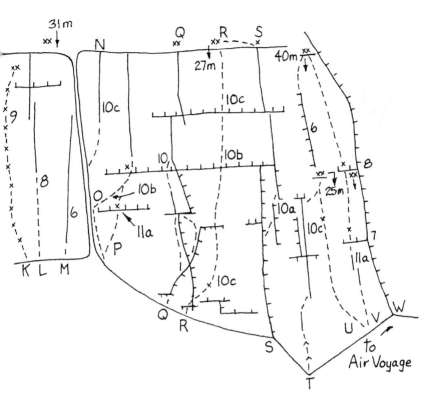

THE AMPHITHEATRE, RIGHT

L	Imaginary Grace**	8	gear to 3"
M	Election Night	6	gear to 4"
N	A Step Away	10c A1	gear to 3"
O	Land's End	10b	gear to 2.5"
P	Polio Roof	11a	gear to 3"
Q	Violet Hour**	10b	gear to 3"
R	Crimson Skies**	10c	gear to 3"
S	Long Stemmed Rose**	10a	gear to 3.5"
T	I Hear My Train A-Comin'**	10c	gear to 3"
U	Mammary Lane	10aR	gear to 3"
V	Slits	11a	gear to 3"
W	Corner Journey**	8	gear to 3"

AIR VOYAGE WALL (OPPOSITE)

A	Corner Journey**	8	gear to 3"
B	Mr Plod**	11c	
C	Mr Rogers Smokes a Fat One**	11b	
C'	Mr Rogers alt. finish**	11c	
D$_1$	Air Voyage P1**	10c	gear to 3"
D$_2$	Air Voyage P2**	11c	gear to 3"
E	Jason Lives**	12d/13a	
F$_1$	Scared Peaches P1**	12a	gear to 2.5"
F$_2$	Scared Peaches P2**	11d	gear to 2.5"
F$_3$	Scared Peaches P3**	11c	gear to 2.5"
G	Scared Shitless*	11d	RPs, small nuts
H$_1$	Where Heathen Rage P1**	12c	small TCUs, 1.5 Friend
H$_2$	Where Geezas Get Amongst It** (Heathen's Extension)	13-	dbl 0, 1 TCUs, Friends to 1.5, RPs small nuts
H'	Heathen's variation*	12c	small TCUs, 1.5 Friend
I	Extra Dry*	9	gear to 3"
J	Manhattan**	12a	
K	DEW Line**	11c	

Note: Take extra care if you lower from the upper Air Voyage, anchor on a 60 m rope; after 30 m you will be level with the top of the big block at the base of the wall, but dangling in space over a 10 m drop to a bad landing! Check that your second is tied to the other end of the rope before you start to lower and have someone ready to pull you in to the top of the block (or clip yourself to the rope that your second is feeding out).

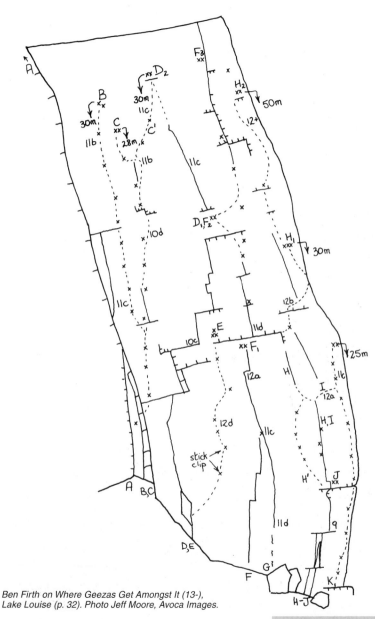

Ben Firth on Where Geezas Get Amongst It (13-), Lake Louise (p. 32). Photo Jeff Moore, Avoca Images.

Ben Firth on When Geezas Get Amongst It (13-), Lake Louise (p32). Photo Jeff Moore, Avoca Images.

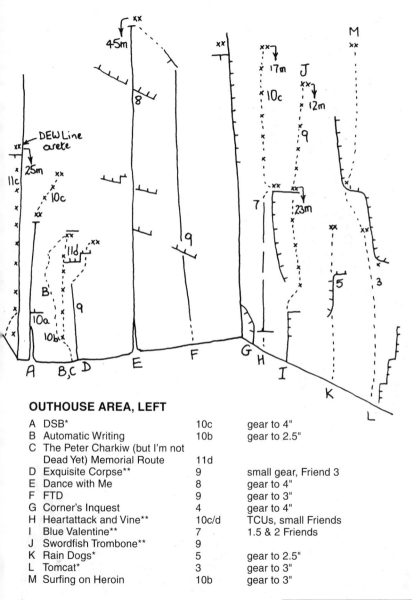

OUTHOUSE AREA, LEFT

A	DSB*	10c	gear to 4"
B	Automatic Writing	10b	gear to 2.5"
C	The Peter Charkiw (but I'm not Dead Yet) Memorial Route	11d	
D	Exquisite Corpse**	9	small gear, Friend 3
E	Dance with Me	8	gear to 4"
F	FTD	9	gear to 3"
G	Corner's Inquest	4	gear to 4"
H	Heartattack and Vine**	10c/d	TCUs, small Friends
I	Blue Valentine**	7	1.5 & 2 Friends
J	Swordfish Trombone**	9	
K	Rain Dogs*	5	gear to 2.5"
L	Tomcat*	3	gear to 3"
M	Surfing on Heroin	10b	gear to 3"

OUTHOUSE, MAIN AREA

A	Tomcat*	3	gear to 3"
B	Female Hands**	12b	
C	Turtle Island*	10b	
D	Ash Wednesday**	10a	gear to 3"
D'	Ash Wednesday var.	10a	gear to 3"
E	Elbows Away**	11b	gear to 3" (inc. 2.5-3 Friend)
F	Venom**	11d	
G	Elbow Venom**	12a	TCUs, long slings
H	Mardi Gras**	11a	
I	project		
J	Purple People Eater*	11c	#2 Rock or TCU
K	Rolling Stone*	10c	gear to 2.5"
L	project		
M	Public Enemy**	10a	
N	Dirty Dancing	12c	
O	Bloodsport**	11b	
P	Top Gun**	7	nuts; 2.5 Friend
Q	Flameout*	10b	
R	Brave New World*	11c/d	med. cam recommended
S	Energizer*	11b/c	
T	Duracell*	10d	
U	Pub Night*	6	gear to 4"
V	Clair's Route	9	

CAUTION: The upper part of this cliff is very steep, so take extra care when lowering/rapping. If you are unfamiliar with the route, back-clip to descend. **You are advised to fix a back rope to descend** *Brave New World*.

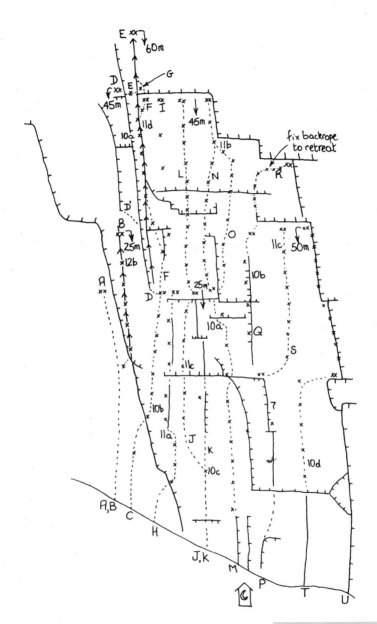

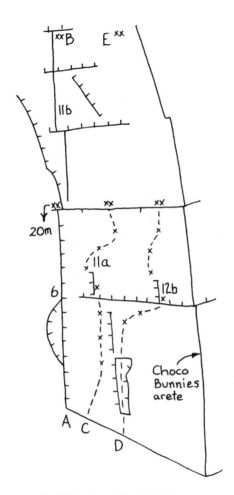

WICKED GRAVITY WALL

A	Pub Night*	6	gear to 4"
B	Monkey Lust*	11b	gear to 4"
C	Wicked Gravity**	11a	
D	Colloidal Impact*	12b	
E	project		

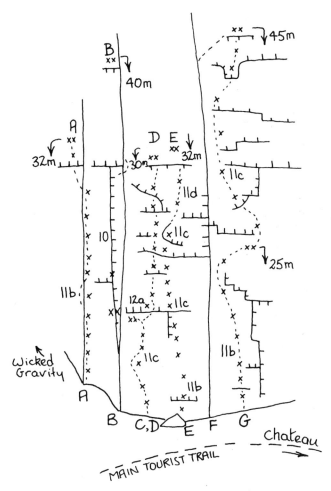

TRAILSIDE

A	Chocolate Bunnies from Hell**	11b	
B	Standing Ovation**	10b/c	gear to 4"
C	Rubber Lover*	11c	
D	Criterium**	12a	
E	Stage Fright**	11d	
F	Another Trailside Attraction**	10b	gear to 4"
G	Aeroflot**	11b, 11c	

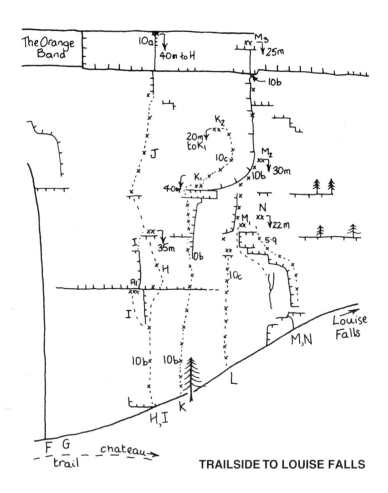

TRAILSIDE TO LOUISE FALLS

H	Darkness at Noon**	10b	
I	Captain Hindgrinder Meets Miss Piggy	10b A1	gear to 3"
J	Room with a View**	10a	gear to 3"
K	Heart of Darkness**	10b, 10b/c	
L	The Incredible Talking Woman**	10c	
M₁	Under Cover* P1	6	gear to 3"
M₂	Under Cover* P2	10b	
M₃	Under Cover* P3	10b	gear to 2"
N	Fiddler on the Roof*	9	

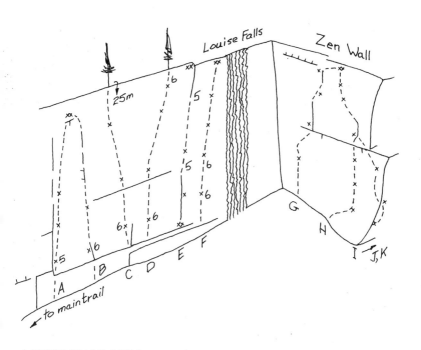

LOUISE FALLS AREA

A	Ryan's Eliminate*	5	small to medium nuts & Friends
B	Pinguicula*	6	"
C	Please Don't Step on the Flowers*	6	"
D	Midget's Mantel**	6	"
E	Cruise Control**	5	"
F	Louise Sticks It**	6	"
G	Crank if You Love Jesus	11b/c	
H	Lords of Karma**	11d R	
I	Zen Arcade**	11c	
J	Rock 102 (not shown)	4	gear to 4"
K	Rock 101 (not shown)	4	gear to 4"

This is a good place to clip bolts on quartzite far from the madding crowds at the Back of the Lake. The cliffs are at an elevation of 2300 m but face south and are dry well before the approach trail is free of snow (often not until July).

Approach

From the Lake Louise parking lot, take the Saddleback Trail to twin cairns at the summit of Saddleback Pass (3.7 km, 600 m elevation gain). Follow a faint trail on the left about 100 m to the low point of the pass at the edge of a hummocky meadow. Now turn right on another faint trail, which descends gently about 100 m to an overlook on the top of a small rock bluff. This is the upper end of Paradise Wall. To get to the routes, downclimb easily to the right and follow the cliff down past two trees growing against the rock.

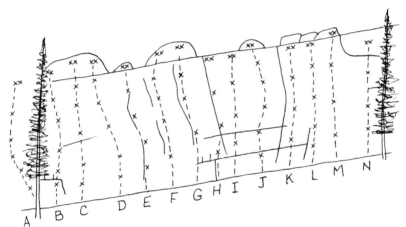

A	Roof of All Evil	11c
B	Young and Modern*	10c/d
C	Big Time*	10d
D	Misfit*	11b
E	Captain Hook*	10c
F	Wandering Jew**	10d
G	Jungle Jenny**	10b
H	Crack of Gloom*	10c
I	Srynx*	11a
J	Toppling Block**	11a
K	Heavy Method*	10d
L	Up for Grabs*	10d
M	Metal Masher*	10c/d
N	Tiny Perfect	10c/d

GRAND SENTINEL (Cardiac Arête)

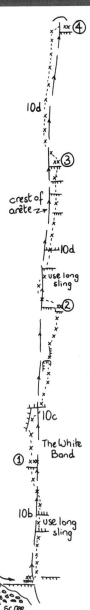

Cardiac Arête, the southeast arête of the Grand Sentinel, is a classy route with lots of atmosphere in a spectacular alpine setting. The climbing is sustained, mostly in the 5.9 to 10a range, with short, clearly defined cruxes. Some rockfall hazard exists, especially if there is a party ahead of you, so wear a helmet. The lower part of the route gets the morning sun while the upper part comes into the sun in the early afternoon. The route is entirely bolt protected (8 - 12 bolts per pitch) and is equipped with chained belay anchors at good ledges. One or two longer slings are useful.

Approach

Follow the trail from Moraine Lake to Sentinel Pass (2611 m) (6 km; 800 m elevation gain). The Grand Sentinel is the largest of several pinnacles situated about 0.5 km to the northwest and the S.E. Arête points directly towards the pass. Descend approximately 35 m via switchbacks on the north side of the pass and then follow a faint trail that contours left (N.W.) across loose scree (snow early in the season) slopes to the notch on the left (W) side of the pinnacle (2 - 2.5 hours from the parking lot). The classic 5.8 route up the Grand Sentinel ascends the face above via the large open book in its centre. Scramble a short distance down the scree gully in front of this face to a narrow, cleaned-off ledge that leads to the right and a 2 bolt belay at the start of the climb. To descend, rap the route (25 m raps).

Warning

In recent years, Parks Canada has imposed travel restrictions and closures in the Sentinel Pass area due to the presence of a grizzly bear. Check the warden's office or the Banff National Park trail report first.

Cardiac Arête**   10d

RAILWAY AVENUE

Railway Avenue is located near Field, B.C., about 100 m west (right) of the ice climb *Cool Spring* on Mount Stephen. The cliff is obvious from the Trans-Canada Highway—100 m above the railroad tracks and about 1 km west of a short railroad tunnel—as a white, roughly circular north-facing patch of steep quartzite, 30 m high, the lower part of which is hidden by trees. A 60 m rope is recommended.

Approach

Park at the parking lot near the beginning of the road to Takakkaw Falls by the Trans-Canada Highway bridge across the Kicking Horse River. Walk up onto the highway, cross the bridge, and then head downstream on the gravel flats on the south side of the Kicking Horse River for a kilometre or so until opposite the *Cool Spring* gully. Hike up through the forest to the tracks, from where the crag is visible again. Cross the tracks about 200 m west of a small trackside cabin and climb a steep, thickly forested slope to the wash-out below *Cool Spring*. Ascend this loose, rocky slope for about 40 m before traversing right and up into more thick forest. Keep traversing gradually right and up to avoid several steep rock steps; then follow a rough steep trail left along the base of the cliffs and scramble the last 10 m to a mossy ledge beneath the climbs. Approach time, about 45 minutes from parking. **Beware of bears!**

WARNING: Do NOT approach by walking along the tracks from Field as this is trespassing. CP Rail employees encountered may be hostile.

RAILWAY AVENUE

A	Choss Your Cookies**	11b
B	Never the Twain**	11a
C	Crippled Herring**	11b/c
D	Whiteman Dancin'***	11b/c
E	Galloping Glaciers**	11c
F	Cranial Hoofprints*	11d

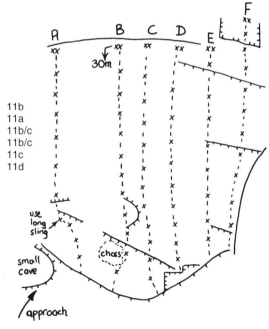

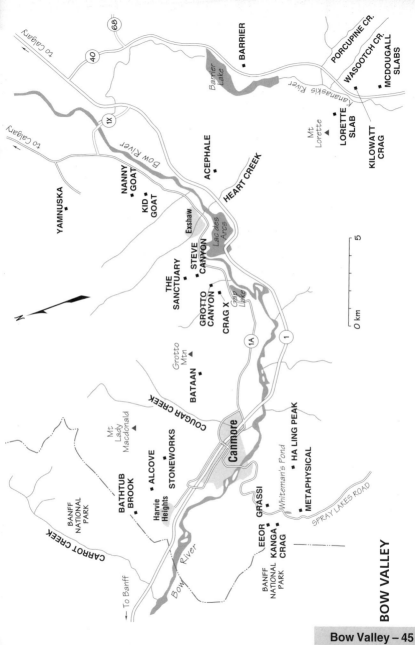

BARRIER

PORCUPINE CR.

WASOOTCH CR.

MCDOUGALL SLABS

to Calgary

68

40

1X

Barrier Lake

Kananaskis River

Mt Lorette

LORETTE SLAB

KILOWATT CRAG

to Calgary

Bow River

NANNY GOAT

KID GOAT

ACEPHALE

HEART CREEK

YAMNUSKA

Exshaw

STEVE CANYON

Lac des Arcs

5

THE SANCTUARY

GROTTO CANYON

CRAG X

Gap Lake

0 km

N

1A

1

Grotto Mtn

BATAAN

COUGAR CREEK

Canmore

HA LING PEAK

Mt Lady Macdonald

ALCOVE

STONEWORKS

Whiteman's Pond

METAPHYSICAL

BATHTUB BROOK

Harvie Heights

GRASSI

SPRAY LAKES ROAD

BANFF NATIONAL PARK

CARROT CREEK

EEOR

KANGA CRAG

BANFF NATIONAL PARK

Bow River

To Banff

To Banff

BOW VALLEY

Bow Valley – 45

This area is located on the north side of Heart Mountain, a pleasant 45 minute walk south of the Trans-Canada Highway. The cliffs abound in very steep, pocketed rock and provide the most difficult climbing to be found in this guidebook, if not in all of Canada. There is not a lot here for the sub-5.12 climber.

The crag comprises a continuous band of rock, several hundred metres long. It is divided into two main climbing areas, Lower Wall and Upper Wall, that are connected by a trail along the base of the cliffs. In addition there are a few climbs on a lower band of rock, Down Under.

Most of Acéphale is in the shade for much of the day and the rock seeps after heavy rainfall, so it is best to wait for warm, dry weather before going there. During light to moderate rain showers, several of the routes stay dry because of the overhanging nature of the rock. The left end of Lower Wall, which faces east and receives morning sunshine, is a popular warm-up area. Down Under stays in the sun until early afternoon.

Approach

Park in the ditch of the eastbound lanes of the Trans-Canada Highway, 1.2 km east of Heart Creek (100 m east of the eastern end of a guard rail). A faint trail above leads to a dip in the embankment and a dry creek bed. Follow this and cross the groomed hiking trail from Heart Creek to Quaite Valley at a bridge. Continue upstream a short distance to a power line. Turn left (east) and follow the trail under the power line for 20 m. The trail now veers right and follows the east (left, looking upstream) side of the drainage. Continue through open woodland, taking the right-hand fork at any branches in the trail, to a beautiful waterfall. Here switchbacks on the left lead to a small slab that is crossed using a fixed chain. The trail now follows the drainage above the waterfall, crossing it several times and leading eventually to a large, dead tree across the dry stream bed near the start of *Ice-cream Head* on Lower Wall.

To reach Down Under, follow the flagged trail that contours right from some slabs in the main Upper Wall trail at the slot cave just uphill from Hypochondria (5 minutes). Or, from the Upper Wall, follow the flagged trail in the trees below *Sweet Thing* for 50 m to a chained rap anchor beside a large tree. Rap 30 m to a rough trail below. The climbs are located about 75 m farther to the right.

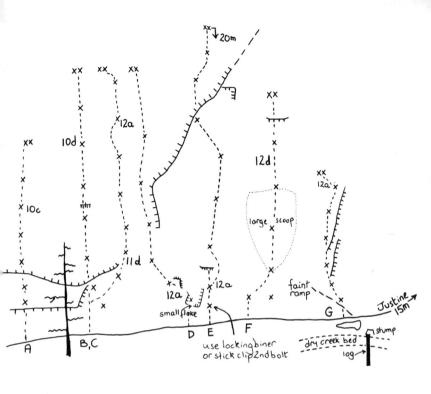

LOWER WALL, LEFT

A	Keys in the Car**	10c
B	Nickel Bag**	10d
C	Girl Drink Drunk**	12a
D	The Irradicator**	12a
E	Illy Down**	12a
F	Ice-Cream Head*	12d
G	Subbacultcha*	12a

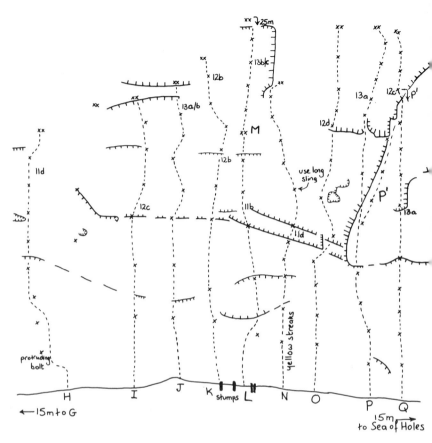

LOWER WALL, RIGHT

H	Justine*	11d
I	La Part Maudite*	12c
J	Naissance de la Femme*	13b
K	Deal With It**	12b/c
L	Neoconstructionist**	11b
M	Wet Lust*	13b/c
N	Where's Mom?*	11d
O	Nemo**	12d
P	The Dark Half**	13a
P'	S.R.16**	12b/c (11+ to first anchor)
Q	Last Dance*	13a

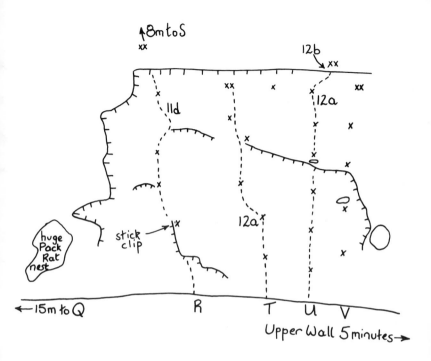

LOWER WALL – SEA OF HOLES

R	Approach Route*	11d	5 more clips to S
S	Pandora*	13b/c	
T	Pluvial Power	12a	
U	Static Dynos	12b	
V	project		

Stefan Butler on Altius (12c), Acephale (p. 52).
Photo Sara Rainford/URBAN COYOTE.

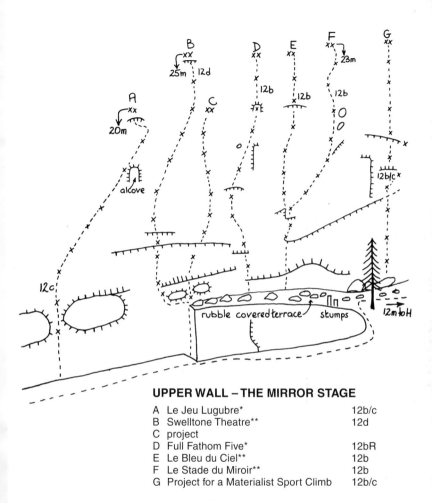

UPPER WALL – THE MIRROR STAGE

A Le Jeu Lugubre*   12b/c
B Swelltone Theatre**   12d
C project
D Full Fathom Five*   12bR
E Le Bleu du Ciel**   12b
F Le Stade du Miroir**   12b
G Project for a Materialist Sport Climb 12b/c

To get to Upper Wall, follow the trail along the base of Lower Wall to the right, down to its low point and then steeply back up (4 - 5 minutes). The next route reached is *Hypochondriac* (12c, 13 clips), which ascends a grey groove a few metres to the right of large cracked corners in a prominent strip of white rock. One minute farther uphill is a large slot cave in rotten rock. 4 m right of the slot cave is a project (10 clips) beneath a prominent dead tree that sticks out into space from the top of the crag. About 40 m right of this is *Le Jeu Lugubre* and the start of Upper Wall.

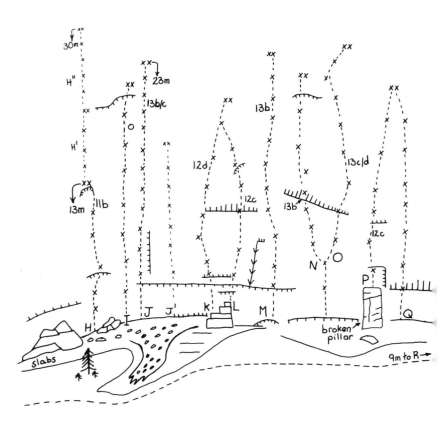

UPPER WALL – BATAILLE

H	Bataille**	11b
H'	Dale's Extender**	11c
H"	The Angry Inch*	13b
I	Porthole to Hell*	13c/d
J	Sweet Thing**	13c
J'	Whale Back**	13c
K	Gingus Americanus (Yankee Go Home)**	12d
L	Copocabana**	12c
M	The Hype**	13b
N	The Hood**	13b
O	Hairballs**	13c/d
P	Altius**	12c
Q	project	

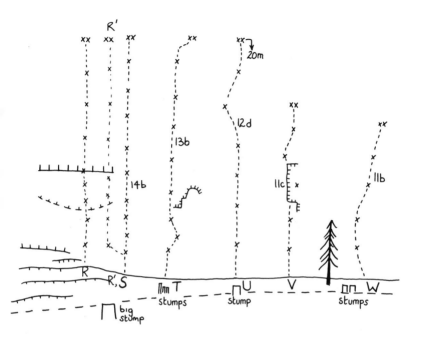

UPPER WALL – THE PAVEMENT

R	Leviathan**	14b
R'	Endless Summer*	13d/14a
S	Existence Mundane	14b
T	Army Ants	13c
U	The 39 Steps	12d/13a
V	La Pause Café	11c
W	Boner	11b

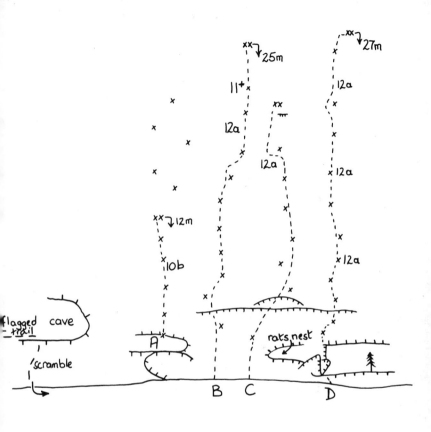

DOWN UNDER

A Pomme*   10b
B Moving Target**   12a/b
C G'day**   12a
D The Wizard of Oz** 12b

*JD LeBlanc on The Hood (13b), Acéphale (p. 52). Photo
Roger Chayer/Talus Photographics.*

HEART CREEK

Heart Creek crosses the Trans-Canada Highway just east of the Lac des Arcs interchange. Because of the narrowness of the valley and the orientation of the cliffs, Heart Canyon tends to be chilly in spring and fall. Jupiter Rock and First Rock get morning sun but go into shade in early afternoon.

Golden Arch Crag and Upper Heart Crag are steep slabs part way up Heart Mountain, just below the ridge trail. Their westerly aspect makes them sunny crags on which one can climb early and late in the season, as long as it is not too windy. The climbing at both crags is technical, rather than strenuous. Two ropes are required for rappelling to the start of the climbs at Upper Heart Crag. Escape from the base of these climbs is easily effected by following the ledge system up and to the right back to the top of the crag.

Approach

The official hiking trail to Heart Creek starts at a parking area located in the southwest quadrant of the Lac des Arcs interchange. Highway signs announce the turn-off. The trail parallels the highway for about 700 m, crosses the creek and then turns right up the creek valley (closed to bicycles from this point on). Most climbers park in the ditch on either side of the highway at the creek crossing and gain the trail from there. This trail provides access to all the valley-bottom climbing areas, ending after about 20 minutes of walking, at the base of Trail's End Cliff.

To get to *Orange on a Window Sill* (10d, 5 bolts, no topo), walk about 200 m up the valley trail to a clearing just beyond a sign that says "Trail Stop 2." Head uphill about 150 m to a rock band. The climb starts behind a large fallen tree.

To reach Golden Arch Crag, walk up the ridge trail to a point across from Jupiter Rock (15 - 20 minutes). Look for a split dead tree just below the ridge at an open bend on the trail. Scramble down a few easy ledges to a sketchy trail that continues across the slope to the crag in about five more minutes. Look for cairns and flagging. There are three routes on half Dome's Bluff, which is just left (south) of the Golden Arch approach, immediately below the ridge crest. *For Aiders Two and Up* (7,4 bolts) starts to the left. The direct start is *Portaledge Posterpedic* (9, A0). To the right is *Pitch 25* (10b, 6 bolts).

To reach Upper Heart Crag, walk up the ridge trail to a small flat area with a large solitary spruce tree (about 40 minutes from the base of the ridge). From here, the main part of the crag can be seen in profile. To reach the five leftmost routes (A-E) traverse at this level along a scree covered ledge to a rappel station at its end. The climbs start at a ledge and ramp system, 30 m below. The remaining routes are reached by continuing up the ridge trail, which climbs steeply past a slabby rib of light grey rock, for a further 3 - 4 minutes. To reach routes F and G, cut over right to a gnarled, live tree and rap chain near the edge. Rap 20 m to the top anchor of route G and then 35 m to its base. The remaining routes are reached by rappelling 45 m from a small ledge, just below the edge, a little higher up the slope from the chained rap tree.

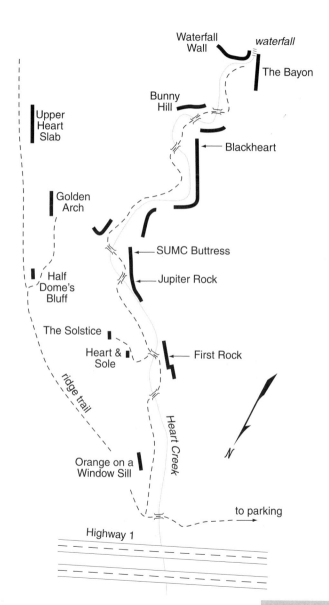

Waterfall Wall

waterfall

The Bayon

Bunny Hill

Blackheart

Upper Heart Slab

Golden Arch

SUMC Buttress

Jupiter Rock

Half Dome's Bluff

The Solstice

Heart & Sole

First Rock

ridge trail

Heart Creek

to parking

Orange on a Window Sill

N

Highway 1

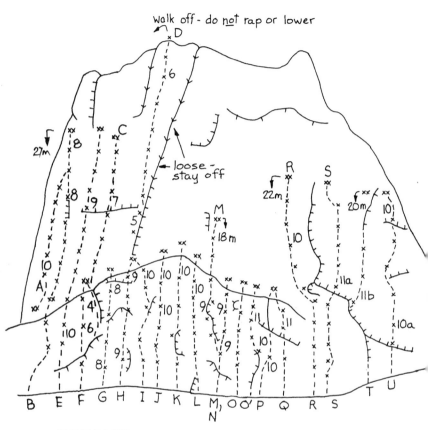

FIRST ROCK

A	Brownout	10c	
B	Potentilla Pillar**	8	
C	Heartline*	7	
D	A Dream of White Schnauzers*	6	do not rap
E	Heartfelt*	10c	
F	Trio	6	
G	Less Than Zero*	8	
H	Back to Zero*	9	
I	Feel On**	10b	
J	Feel On Baby**	10b	
K	Dynamic Dumpling*	10d/11a	

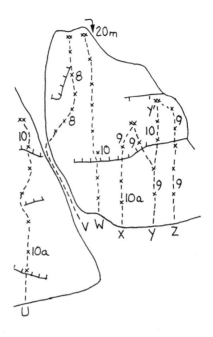

FIRST ROCK

L	Survival of the Fattest**	10c	
M	Cavebird**	9	
N	Pyramid Power**	9	
O	Midnight Rambler*	10c	
O'	Sweet Souvenir	11c	
P	Honky Tonk Woman	10c	gear to Friend 3
Q	Voodoo Lounge*	11c	
R	Let it Bleed**	10a	
S	Paint it Black*	11a	
T	Bitch*	11b	gear to Friend 3
U	Sticky Fingers**	10c	
V	Dandelions**	8	
W	Dead Flowers*	10b	
X	Brown Sugar*	10a	
Y	Heartburn	9	
Y'	Heartburn Direct*	10c	
Z	Wild Horses	9	

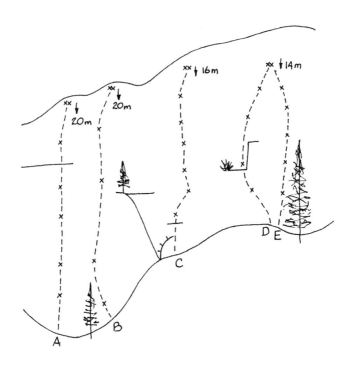

THE SOLSTICE

From Heart & Soul, follow a trail right and up for about 3 minutes.

A Electric Koolaid Ocean   6
B Herbivore Dance   5
C Iron Eclipse   8
D Tribal Wedding   9
E Merry Pranksters   10a

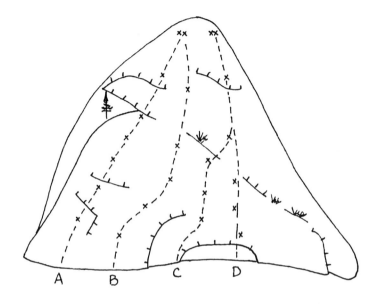

HEART & SOLE

From first rock, cross the bridge and immediately turn left on a trail 3 - 4 minutes up to the cliff.

A	Itchy Jig	7
B	Sole Food	9
C	Heart & Sole	9
D	Mr Percival	10a

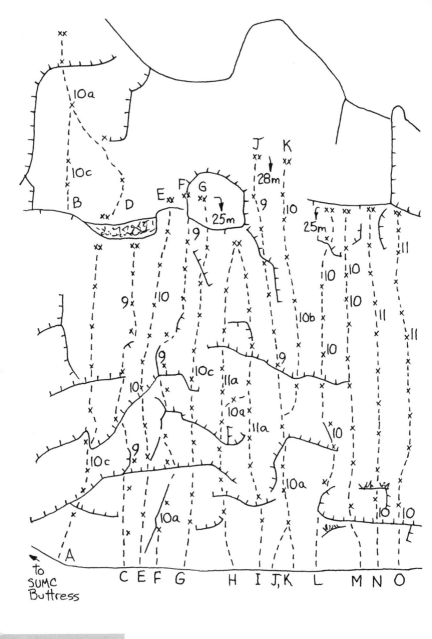

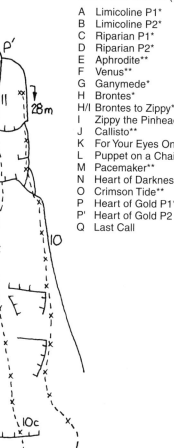

JUPITER ROCK (opposite)

A	Limicoline P1*	10c	
B	Limicoline P2*	10c	
C	Riparian P1*	9	
D	Riparian P2*	10a	
E	Aphrodite**	10b	
F	Venus**	10a	
G	Ganymede*	10c	
H	Brontes*	11a	
H/I	Brontes to Zippy**	10a	
I	Zippy the Pinhead*	11a	
J	Callisto**	10a	
K	For Your Eyes Only**	10b	
L	Puppet on a Chain**	10c	
M	Pacemaker**	10c	
N	Heart of Darkness**	11b	
O	Crimson Tide**	11a/b	
P	Heart of Gold P1*	10c	
P'	Heart of Gold P2	11a	gear; no anchors
Q	Last Call	10a/b	

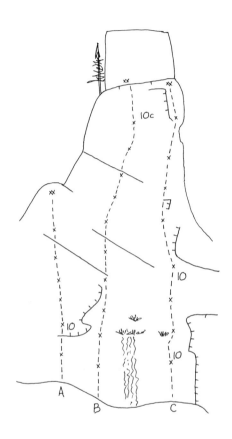

SUMC BUTTRESS

A Glide   10b
B Original Route 10c
C Illusive Edge 10b

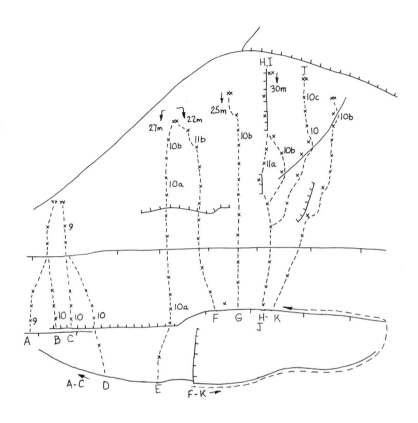

BLACKHEART

A	Half a Heart	9
B	Kiss and Tell	10a
C	Have a Heart	10a
D	Shoot from the Hip	10a
E	Heart Throb**	10b
F	Bleeding Heart*	11b
G	Braveheart**	10b
H	Blackheart Direct*	11a
I	Blackheart*	10b
J	Heart of Stone*	10c
K	Heartbreaker*	10b

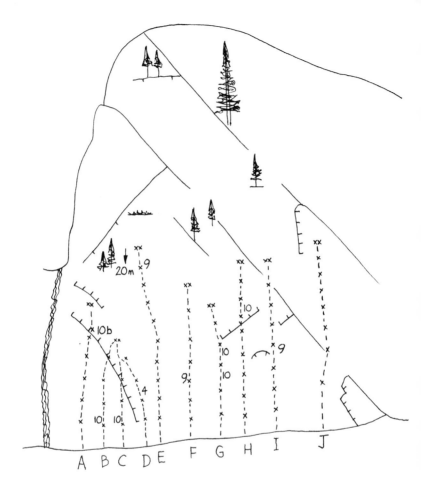

BUNNY HILL

A	Heartless*	10b
B	Rat in a Cage	10a
C	Chip Butty	10a
D	Simple*	4
E	You Oughtta Know**	9+
F	Come As You Are*	9
G	Until it Sleeps*	10d
H	Contemporary Cuisine*	10b
I	Rough But Well Groomed*	9+
J	Carpe Diem*	10c/d

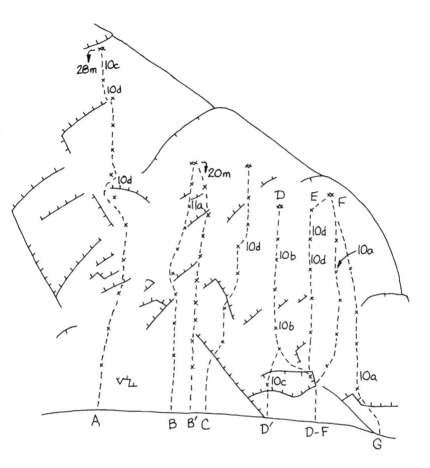

28m 10c

10d

10d

20m

11a

10d

10b

D E F

10d

10d

10b

10d

10a

10b

10c

10a

10a

A B B' C D' D-F G

WATERFALL WALL

A	Omnivore**	10d
B	Trail's End**	11a
B'	Masterbretter	11b
C	Les Nuages*	10d
D	Lazarus*	10b
D'	Lazarus Direct*	10c
E	Stretchmarks**	10d
F	Downdraft*	10a
G	Gridlock	10a

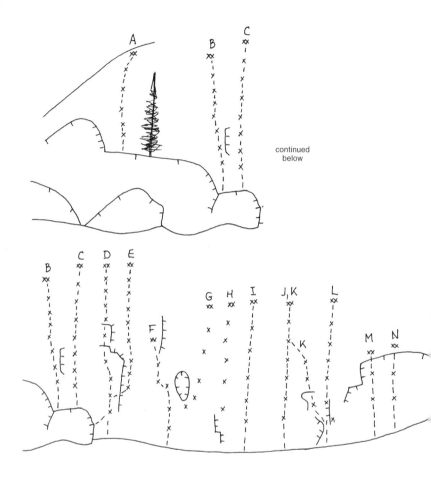

continued below

THE BAYON

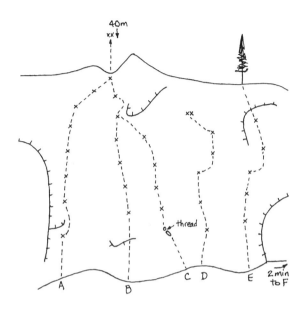

GOLDEN ARCH CRAG

A Bones on the Moon   10c
B Gerg Lenrock Pounds Mr Slate   10d
C Harder than Ron Jeremy   11a
D Interview with the CMC Vampire   10c/d
E 1970s Rock Olympics   10c
F For Sportbras and Pantilines   8
G Gumboot Cloggeroo   10a/b
H The Drill Sergeant   10a
I Fiddles over Kandahar   8

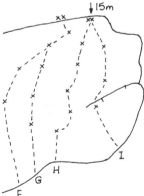

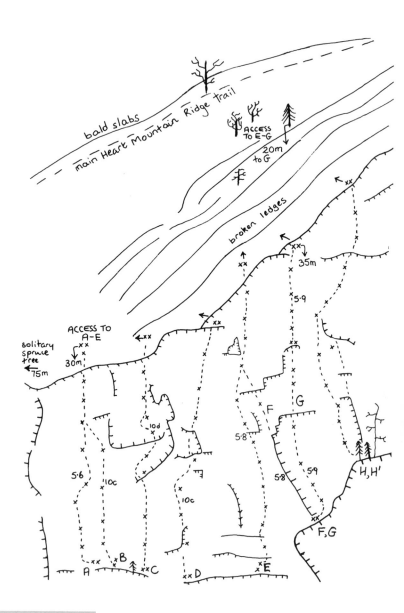

bald slabs

main Heart Mountain Ridge trail

ACCESS TO E-G

20m to G

broken ledges

35m

5·9

ACCESS TO A-E

30m

solitary spruce tree

75m

10d

5·6

10c

10c

5·8

F

G

5·8

5·8

5·9

H, H'

A   B   C   D   E   F, G

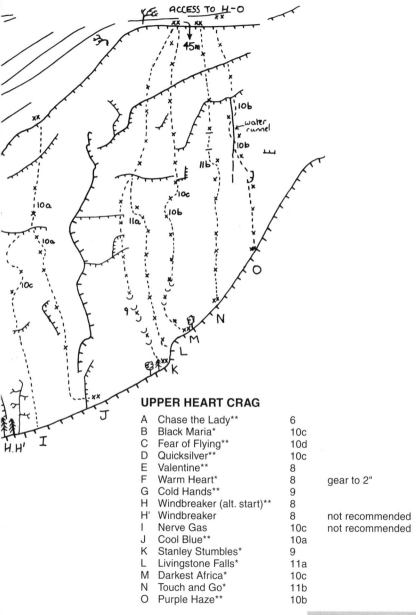

UPPER HEART CRAG

A	Chase the Lady**	6	
B	Black Maria*	10c	
C	Fear of Flying**	10d	
D	Quicksilver**	10c	
E	Valentine**	8	
F	Warm Heart*	8	gear to 2"
G	Cold Hands**	9	
H	Windbreaker (alt. start)**	8	
H'	Windbreaker	8	not recommended
I	Nerve Gas	10c	not recommended
J	Cool Blue**	10a	
K	Stanley Stumbles*	9	
L	Livingstone Falls*	11a	
M	Darkest Africa*	10c	
N	Touch and Go*	11b	
O	Purple Haze**	10b	

The impressive north face of Ha Ling Peak (aka Chinaman's Peak) is a prominent Canmore landmark that boasts the longest limestone sport climb north of Mexico. *Sisyphus Summits* is fully equipped and all station-to-station rappels can be done with one 50 m rope. After pitch 1, pitches can be combined and climbed as 50 m pitches. Pitches 19, 20 and 21 can be combined as a single 60 m pitch. Don't take this route lightly just because it's "only" 5.10—competent parties can expect to take about 7 hours. Take sturdy running shoes for the descent and **WEAR A HELMET**, as parts of the route are subject to rockfall from the popular (but loose) Northeast Buttress route.

Approach
From Canmore, drive up the Spray Lakes Road (when approaching from the east on the TransCanada Highway, it saves about 5 minutes to take Three Sisters Drive to the Spray Lakes Road) a short distance past the dam that impounds Whiteman's Pond. Park at a lakeside parking area. Walk back to the dam and cross it. Climb around a gated section, and follow a trail up right through the trees. Soon, cut up left toward the face and, as the trees start to thin, locate a trail that angles up right toward broken cliffs at the west end of the face. Climb scree slopes and gain a trail at the base of the face. Follow this left to a cairn at the base of the route.

Descent
The most common route down is to descend the trail on the southwest side of the mountain. Head south from the summit to a col and continue on a good trail that leads down to a bridge across the diversion canal at the foot of the mountain and thence to the Spray Lakes Road, about 800 m from the parking area. Alternatively, scramble down slabs in the cirque to the east of the peak and thus return to the base of the route. Rappelling the route is the slowest option and is not recommended.

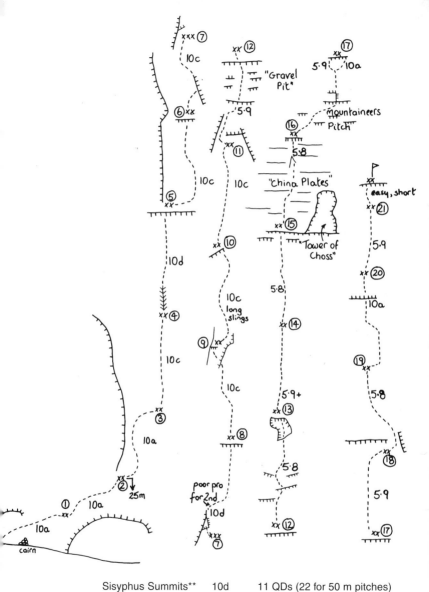

Sisyphus Summits**   10d   11 QDs (22 for 50 m pitches)

VIAGRA POINT

Viagra Point is a steep yellow wall at the highest point of the cliff band that extends westward from below Ha Ling Peak.

A Cunning Linguist   11a/b
B Dirk Diggler   11b/c

Approach

Approach via the trail to Sisyphus Summits. The climbs start just right of a single tree growing close to the face and about 10 m left of the edge of the forest. Rappel to descend (2 ropes needed).

Grassi Lakes offers climbing on steep, pocketed rock through a wide range of grades. Many of the routes are designed to be **stick-clipped**. Note that there is **rockfall hazard** at all the northside cliffs from careless tourists and also from bighorn sheep.

Approach

Drive up the Spray Lakes Road from Canmore (or, when driving from the east, take Three Sisters Drive to the Spray Lakes Road) to the top of the hill (about 6.5 km from downtown) and park at Whiteman's Pond (as for Ha Ling Peak). Obey "No Parking" signs. Descend at the edge of the dam into a picturesque gorge. Within a couple of minutes you will pass under a steep cliff on the left. This is The Ghetto. Another minute or so down a trail will take you past The Rectory to a level area with small cliffs on both sides, the Swamp Buttress Area. Continue about 1 minute more through a tumbled mass of large boulders to reach the White Imperialist Area, beside the trail on your left. Hermit Wall is the large, north-facing cliff across the valley at this point. Another 3 minutes or so down the gorge is a steep, rubbly slope leading down to the upper Grassi Lake. At this point you will just have passed a route on your left, *Real Good Time* (10a, 6 clips). *Lemming* (11c, 4 clips) is on a small buttress to the right, the Mole Hill. The cliff ahead of you on the right is Gardener's Wall, a steep pocketed cliff that features some closely-bolted routes suitable for beginning leaders; ahead and left are The Golf Course, a low angled slab popular with beginners (partway down the rubbly slope mentioned above); and beyond that the Meathooks Area (near the base of the slope on a short, very overhanging wall). The Graceland Area overlooks the lake on the north side.

This route description presumes that TransAlta Utilities, the landowner, will continue to allow access from the dam. If not, a signed hiking trail can be used to access Grassi Lakes from below. Look for a turn-off where the pavement ends, just beyond the Canmore Nordic Centre.

An owl nests each year in a cave just left of the Graceland Area (p. 87). Alberta Environment may post signage of a restricted area during nesting season. The climbs involved are *You Ain't Nothing but a Hang Dog*, *Memphis* and *Graceland*. Please stay off these climbs during the restricted period to avoid disturbing the owls. FAILURE TO RESPECT THE ALBERTA ENVIRONMENT REQUEST COULD LEAD TO PERMANENT CLOSURE OF THIS AREA OF THE CLIFF (and make climbers look bad in the eyes of the public).

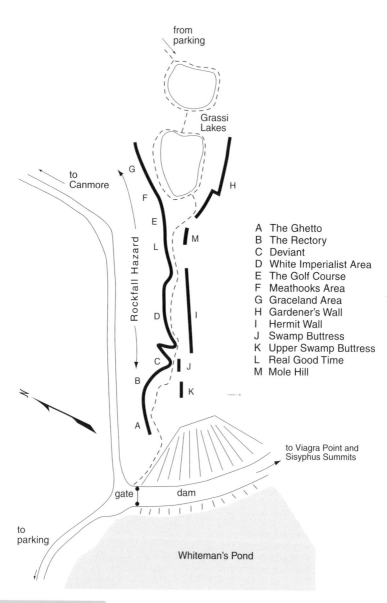

A The Ghetto
B The Rectory
C Deviant
D White Imperialist Area
E The Golf Course
F Meathooks Area
G Graceland Area
H Gardener's Wall
I Hermit Wall
J Swamp Buttress
K Upper Swamp Buttress
L Real Good Time
M Mole Hill

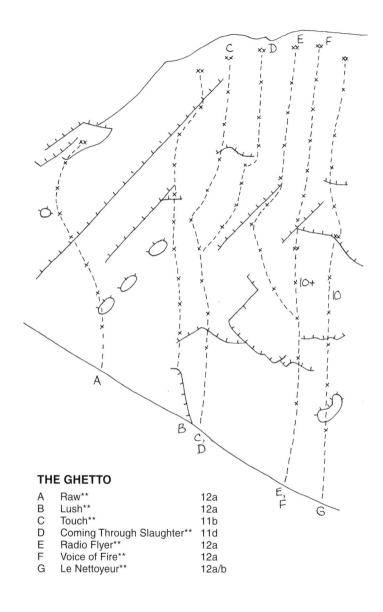

THE GHETTO

A	Raw**	12a
B	Lush**	12a
C	Touch**	11b
D	Coming Through Slaughter**	11d
E	Radio Flyer**	12a
F	Voice of Fire**	12a
G	Le Nettoyeur**	12a/b

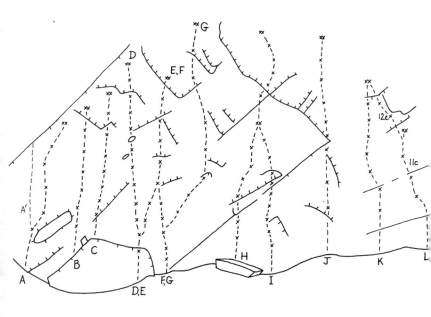

THE RECTORY

A'	The Scourge	12a/b R/X	#1TCU; med cams
A	Two Different Worlds	12b	
B	Blood of Eden**	12a	
C	Soft Machine**	11c	
D	Cool Sensations**	12a	
E	Blunt**	12a/b	
F	Blunt Direct**	12c	
G	The Gimp	12d	
H	project		
I	Full Tilt**	12c/d	
J	Nice Try	12d	
K	Massive Attack**	12c	
L	Fuel**	12c	

Jenna Rae Puscus (age 8) climbing at the Golf Course, Grassi Lakes. Photo Jacquie Puscus.

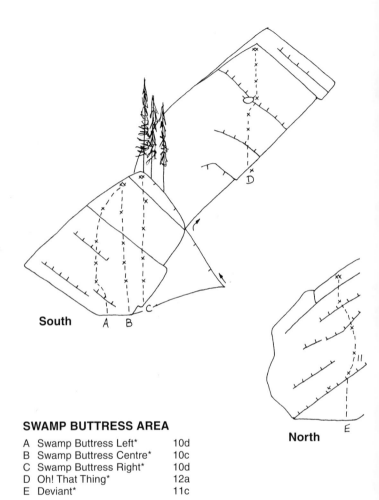

South

A B C

North

E

SWAMP BUTTRESS AREA

A	Swamp Buttress Left*	10d
B	Swamp Buttress Centre*	10c
C	Swamp Buttress Right*	10d
D	Oh! That Thing*	12a
E	Deviant*	11c

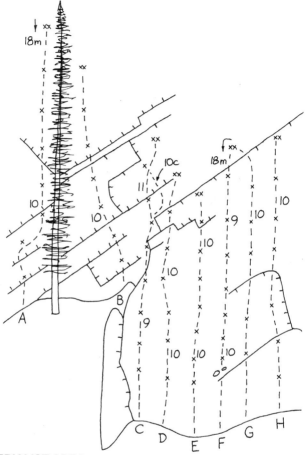

WHITE IMPERIALIST AREA

A	Carom*	10b
B	Spin*	10b
C	Pink Flamingos*	10c or 11a
D	White Imperialist**	10d
E	Yellow Peril**	10b
F	Golden Horde**	10a
G	Red Menace**	10c
H	Dark Design**	10b
I	Gizmo*	8
J	Homer Downs a Duff*	7
K	Johnny Mnemonic*	10a

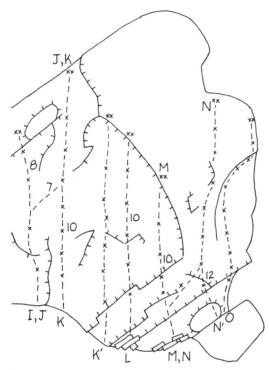

WHITE IMPERIALIST, RIGHT

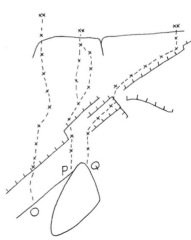

HERMIT WALL

A	Cold Fusion*	10d/11a
B	Dakar**	11d
C	Silk**	10d; 11a/b
D	Ain't It Hell**	10d; 11b
E	The Eyes Have It*	10b or 11a
F	Say It Ain't So*	10c
G	Mr Manners**	11a
H	open project	
I	Green Room*	11a
J	Cry Wolf*	10c (at right end of cliff)

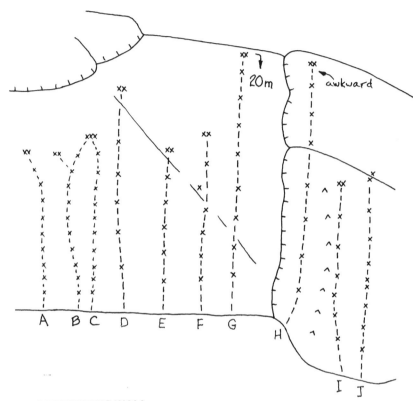

GARDENER'S WALL

A	Lumpy Lane*	9	(kiddy route)
B	Pothole Alley*	9	(kiddy route)
C	Rocky Road*	9	(kiddy route)
D	Gardener's Question Time**	9	
E	Pocket Full of Worms**	9	
F	Horrorculture*	8	
G	I Must Mention Gentians**	10a	
H	Weed 'Em and Reap	10b	
I	Bucket City**	10b	
J	Fiberglass Undies**	10c	

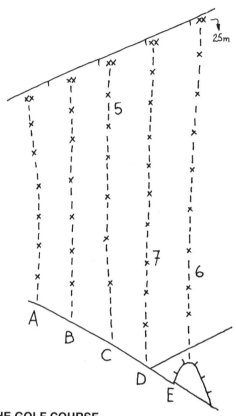

THE GOLF COURSE

A Tiger   5
B Elk Don't Golf   5
C I'd Rather Be Golfing*   5
D Hole in One*   7
E Chip Shot*   6

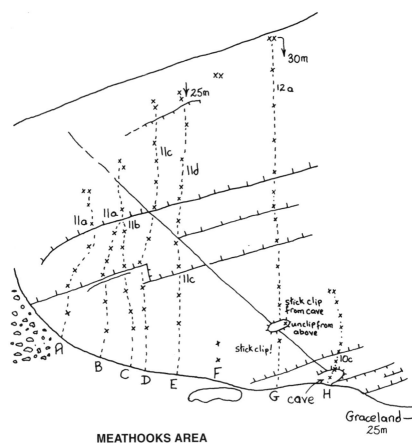

MEATHOOKS AREA

A	Choss Toss**	10d/11a
B	Meathooks**	11a
C	Stormtroopers in Drag**	11b
D	Holey Shit**	11c
E	The Harlot**	11d
F	project	
G	B60 OFO (AKA Thirty Something)**	12a
H	Born from the Mountain	10c

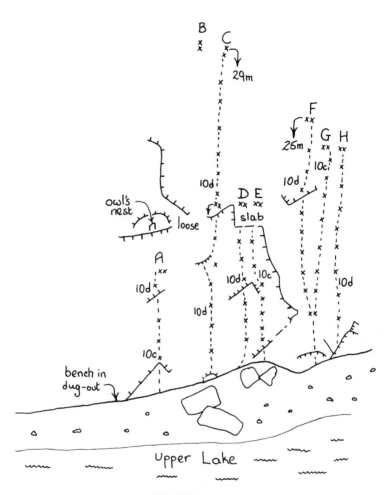

GRACELAND AREA

A You Ain't Nothin' but a Hang Dog* 10d
B project
C Memphis**   10d
D Graceland**   10d
E Elvis Lives**   10c
F Heartbreak Hotel*   10d
G Sunglasses & Sideburns**   10c
H Honeymoon in Vegas**   10d

Lynda Howard on Meathooks (11a), Grassi Lakes (p. 86). Photo John Martin.

KANGA CRAG AND EEOR

Approach

Follow the Spray Lakes Road south from Canmore (or, when driving from the east, take Three Sisters Drive to the Spray Lakes Road) to the parking area at Whiteman's Pond (as for Ha Ling Peak). A trail on the other side of the road follows a sparsely treed, shallow depression up the hill to Kanga Crag, reaching it at *Rocky & Me* (10 - 12 minutes). To get to EEOR, follow the trail past the right end of Kanga Crag and directly across a talus slope. The prominent triangular roof marked on the topo of EEOR will now be clearly visible. A short, steep section of trail leads up beside a large scree chute, which is crossed near its apex to reach the base of the climbs (20 - 25 minutes from the parking area). Headbangers Rock, a large boulder on the trail to Kanga, has two routes: *The Banger in Tights* (5.8, 3 bolts) on the left; *Feathered Hair* (11a/b, 4 bolts) on the right.

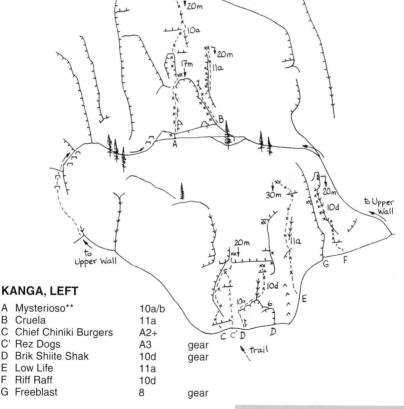

KANGA, LEFT

A	Mysterioso**	10a/b	
B	Cruela	11a	
C	Chief Chiniki Burgers	A2+	
C'	Rez Dogs	A3	gear
D	Brik Shiite Shak	10d	gear
E	Low Life	11a	
F	Riff Raff	10d	
G	Freeblast	8	gear

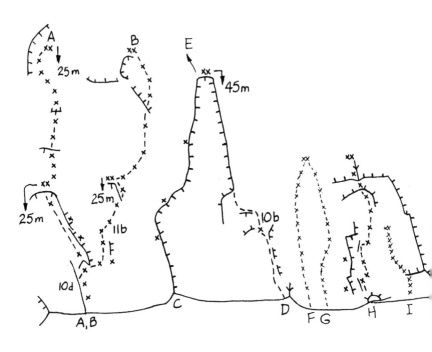

KANGA, MAIN WALL LEFT

A	Canadian Air	12a	
B	Leave Your Hat On	12a	
C	Canadian Cookie	9/10a	gear to 5"
D	California Dreaming	10b	gear to 3"
E	Alberta Reality**	11c, 10a	
F	Roo'd Awakening	11b	gear to 3"
G	Tourette's Syndrome	11a	
H	The Final Battle	A3+	thin gear, bathooks
I	Silent Partner	A1	bolt ladder

*CLIMBERS ARE STONGLY ADVISED TO WEAR HELMETS
WHEN CLIMBING ON EITHER KANGA CRAG OR EEOR
BECAUSE OF ROCKFALL HAZARD*

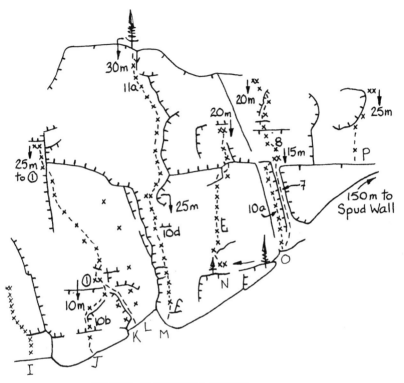

KANGA, MAIN WALL RIGHT

J	Fowl Play	10b	
K	Superior Cackling Chickens*	10b	
L	project		
M	Rocky & Me**	11a	
N	Rub Me Right**	10b	
O	Toucha Toucha Me	8 or 10a	
P	Pit Bull Terr-EEOR	9	small gear

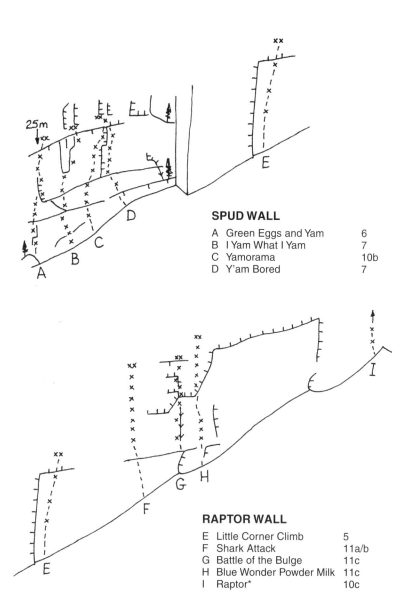

SPUD WALL

A Green Eggs and Yam   6
B I Yam What I Yam   7
C Yamorama   10b
D Y'am Bored   7

RAPTOR WALL

E Little Corner Climb   5
F Shark Attack   11a/b
G Battle of the Bulge   11c
H Blue Wonder Powder Milk   11c
I Raptor*   10c

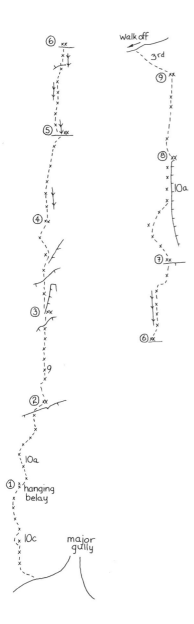

Raptor*   10c

Raptor is immediately left of the huge gully at the left end of EEOR. Approach as for EEOR. Although *Raptor* is rigged as a sport route, it has some loose rock, particularly on ledges. **A helmet is strongly recommended.** Please don't rap the route if there is a party below you. Instead, walk down the ridge to descend. When it levels off, cut left (cairn) down treed slopes and cliff bands (easy downclimbing) to join the ascent path. Alternatively, continue down the ridge and where it drops off steeply, turn left on a trail down steep forested slopes to reach the road.

Parallel Dreams and *True Grit* are a short distance right of the huge gully near *Raptor*. To find the routes, look for a prominent corner capped by a large roof that casts a distinctive triangular shadow when in the sun. This feature is just right of the large terrace at the top of the first two pitches.

Climbers on *True Grit* will encounter a bewildering array of anchor stations. Some of these are for belays, some for a 25 m rap route, some for a 50 m rap route and one is for a traditional route, *Geriatric*. Rap stations are denoted by R on the topo. The Geriatric station is denoted by G. **WARNING**: to descend by 25 m raps (not recommended) you **must** rap from R2 to G4 and then **downclimb** to regain *True Grit* at station 3. We recommend using one 60 m or two 50 m ropes.

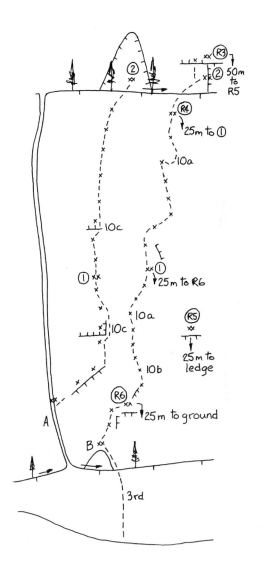

Averyl McDonald on True Grit
(10b), EEOR (p. 95).
Photo Jeff Moore/Avoca Images.

A   Parallel Dreams**   10d/11a
B   True Grit**   10b or 10c

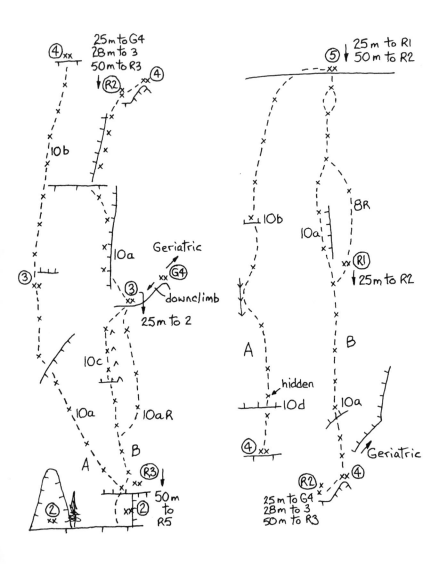

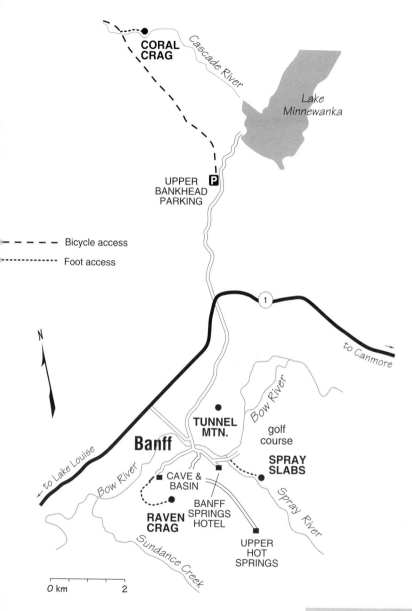

CORAL CRAG

Cascade River

Lake Minnewanka

UPPER BANKHEAD PARKING **P**

– – – Bicycle access

.... Foot access

N

1

to Canmore

to Lake Louise

Bow River

Banff

TUNNEL MTN.

Bow River

golf course

SPRAY SLABS

CAVE & BASIN

BANFF SPRINGS HOTEL

RAVEN CRAG

Spray River

UPPER HOT SPRINGS

Sundance Creek

_0 km_   2

RAVEN CRAG

This steep, northwest-facing crag is situated on the northwest end of the Sulphur Mountain ridge behind the Cave and Basin Pool.

Approach
The approach to Raven Crag takes an indirect route to avoid a wildlife closure area. From the Cave and Basin follow the paved path toward Sundance Canyon. Go left on the first wide horse trail for 200 m, then left on a flagged footpath up to and along the ridge (which defines the western boundary of the wildlife closure area) until level with the cliff (obvious). Traverse left to the cliff. Total time about 30 minutes.

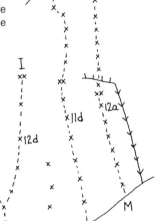

down & around
15m to A

A	The Raven**	10d	2 pitches (35m, 25m); 10 QDs
B	The Hermit	13a/b	
C	One Robe, One Bowl	12b/c	
D-E	projects		
F	Overlooking Paradise**	12c	
G	project		
H	House of Usher*	12a	
I	Tales of Mystery	12d	
J	project		
K	The Masque, P1*	11d	
L	The Masque, P2	12d/13a	
M	Telltale Heart, P1**	12a	
N	Telltale Heart, P2**	13a	

SPRAY SLABS

Formed from steeply tilted siltstone of the Sulphur Mountain Formation, this unusual cliff offers short, technical edging problems on tiny holds. Cool temperatures and low humidity are important ingredients of success on the harder climbs. The routes lacking top anchors or with inadequate protection are not recommended for leading.

Approach
From the Bow Falls parking lot, cross the Spray River on the bridge leading to the golf course. Skirt the first fairway on the riverbank and pick up a trail. Follow this about 10 minutes to the slabs, which are beside the trail, just past a footbridge. See map on page 97.

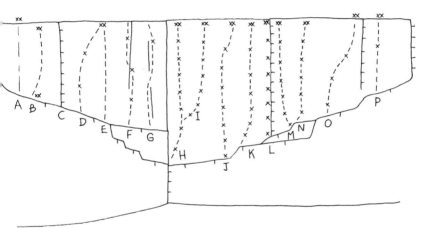

A	unnamed	11a
B	Rampant Orifice	11a
C	unnamed	10a
D	Louisiana Red	10c
E	Sweet Georgia Brown	11c
F	Fear of Flying	11b
G	Bad Sneakers	10c
H	The Graduate*	10d
I	Heavy Metal**	10c
J	Nine Below Zero*	11a
K	Half Deck**	10c
L	Union Maid**	10a
M	Aleutian Chain**	10b
N	Johnny Three-Fingers*	10b
O	Halloween*	10d
P	Saddle Sniffer	10d

A few sport climbing routes have recently been developed on the east side of Tunnel Mountain near the north end. They include 1-pitch routes on the first tier of cliffs (Industrial Playground), 1-pitch routes on the third tier (Personal Pleasures) and a 3-pitch route (Funky Town).

Approach

From downtown Banff, turn east off Banff Avenue on Wolf Street. After a few blocks turn left on Otter Street (signage for Tunnel Mountain Campground). Follow Otter Street up a long hill on the north side of Tunnel Mountain. At the top of the hill, continue past Buffalo Mountain Lodge on the right and turn right on Tunnel Mountain Drive. After 300 m there is a winter closure gate. Park at the first pull-out on the left, at the first bend in the road beyond the gate. Head left up a steep trail straight to the base of the rock. For Industrial Playground, follow a trail at the base of the cliffs left to the climbing routes. Continue up and left along the base of the rock to get to Funky Town. For Personal Pleasures, head up steep terrain to the right (from the point at which you reach the base of the cliffs), climbing rock and roots and trees to a ledge at the base of the third tier of cliffs.

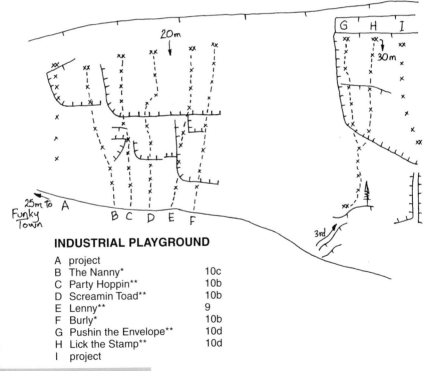

INDUSTRIAL PLAYGROUND

A	project	
B	The Nanny*	10c
C	Party Hoppin**	10b
D	Screamin Toad**	10b
E	Lenny**	9
F	Burly*	10b
G	Pushin the Envelope**	10d
H	Lick the Stamp**	10d
I	project	

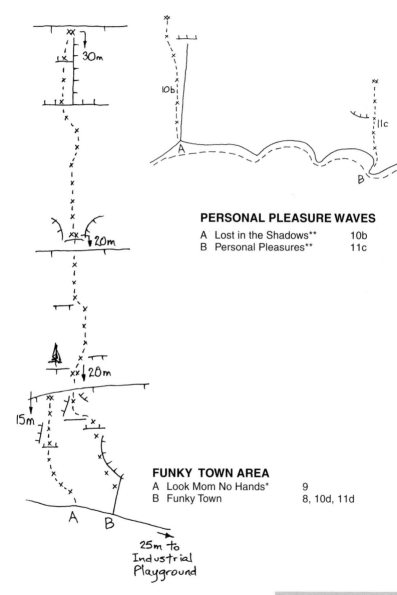

PERSONAL PLEASURE WAVES

A	Lost in the Shadows**	10b
B	Personal Pleasures**	11c

FUNKY TOWN AREA

A	Look Mom No Hands*	9
B	Funky Town	8, 10d, 11d

25m to
Industrial
Playground

Two 4-pitch sport climbs have been completed on the south-facing cliff seen from the Sunshine parking lot. This is the cliff on which the *Bourgeau Left Hand* and *Right Hand* ice climbs form.

Approach

Take the Sunshine Ski Area turn-off approximately 12 km west of Banff. Follow the road to its end at a large parking lot. From the parking lot follow Healy Creek by way of a faint trail up through a poplar grove. Above this, climb an open hillside and several short cliff bands toward a waterfall at the left side of a large gray wall. At the base of the cliffs, traverse around to the right about 60 m. Look for a major left facing corner (*Italian Birdcage Maker*, 5.8+, 3 pitches, gear) and continue to a small, J-shaped tree at its base (see topo). Bring 10 QDs and sunscreen (south facing, high elevation) and a 55 m or 60 m rope for rapping.

Mount Bourgeau cliffs.   A Flirting with the Bosch**, B Walk of Ages*. Photo Chris Perry.

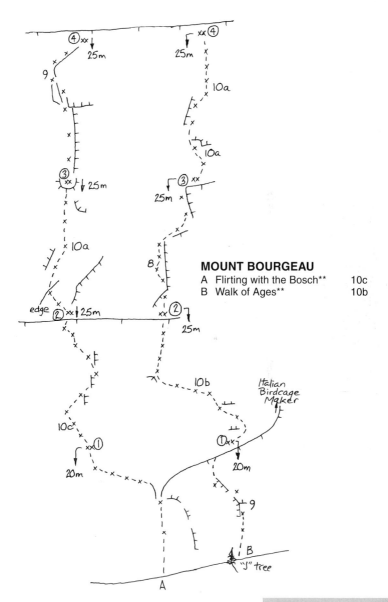

MOUNT BOURGEAU

A Flirting with the Bosch**   10c
B Walk of Ages**   10b

4 xx ↓ 25m

9

3 xx ↓ 25m

10a

edge 2 xx ↓ 25m

10c

1 xx ↓ 20m

xx 4 ↓ 25m

10a

10a

3 xx ↓ 25m

8

2 xx ↓ 25m

10b

Italian Birdcage Maker

1 xx ↓ 20m

9

B "J" tree

A

Approach

Leave the Trans Canada Highway at the Bow Valley Parkway (Highway 1A) exit, 4 km west of Banff, and drive toward Johnston Canyon for 3.2 km to a viewpoint and parking area on the left. A good trail zigzags steeply up the hillside directly across the road to a bench and then angles up slightly left toward the crag. Upon reaching a dry watercourse, either angle up right to the base of a lower angled area (Take It for Granite Area) or continue up easy, broken rock just left of the watercourse to a bowl about 15 m below the steep main cliff. Follow a faint trail left across a rocky rib and traverse horizontally left above broken slabs for about 50 m to some well-used ledges that undercut the base of the cliff. The classic traditional route *The Three Roofs* begins behind a large tree on the right and the bolt belay for *Sea of Dreams* is at the upper left end of the ledges.

Guides Rock. 1. Sea of Dreams, 2. Hurricane, 3. Take it for Granite. Photo Chris Perry.

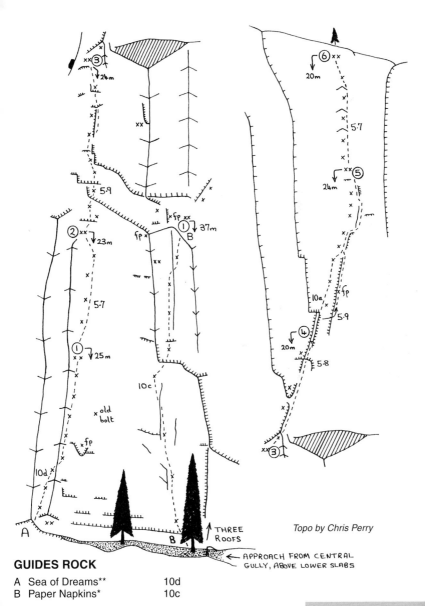

Topo by Chris Perry

GUIDES ROCK

A Sea of Dreams**   10d
B Paper Napkins*   10c

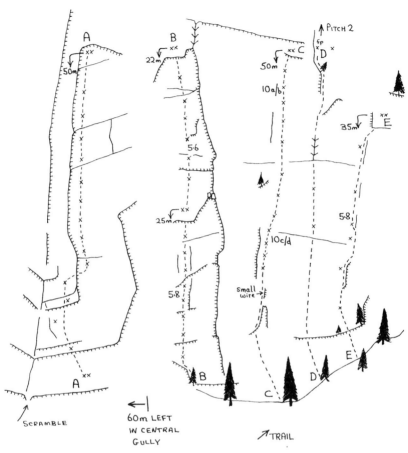

Topo by Chris Perry

TAKE IT FOR GRANITE

A	Hurricane*	11c	
B	Cheese Grater	7/8	small wires useful
C	Take It or Leave It**	10c/d	
D	Take It for Granite*	9	small to med gear
E	For Sure*	8	

CORAL CRAG

This cliff, formed by a series of near-vertical bedding plane slabs, is a few kilometres north of Banff in a secluded location on the bank of the Cascade River. The climbs tend to be technical and the cruxes of the harder routes often involve micro-edge cranks. The cliff faces southwest and gets afternoon sun.

Approach
Drive north along the Lake Minnewanka Road and park at the Upper Bankhead picnic area, which also serves as the trailhead for the Cascade Fire Road. Bicycle along the road to a bridge across the Cascade River (5.6 km). Cross the river, park your bike, and walk downstream on a faint trail for about 10 minutes to the cliff.

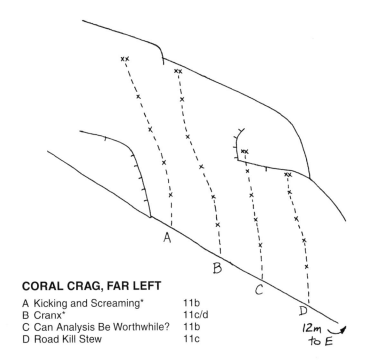

CORAL CRAG, FAR LEFT

A Kicking and Screaming*   11b
B Cranx*   11c/d
C Can Analysis Be Worthwhile?   11b
D Road Kill Stew   11c

12m
to E

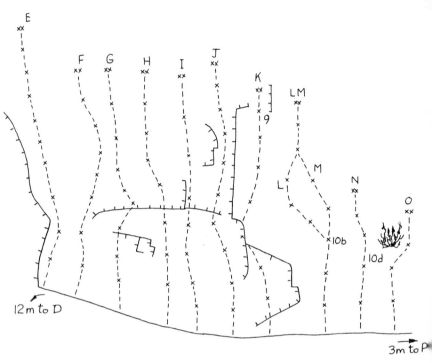

CORAL CRAG, LEFT

E	Rusty Piton Route**	8
F	Tumbelina*	11c
G	Toxic Trout*	11b
H	Deadman's Party*	11d
I	Powder Monkey*	11c/d
J	Duration Gluttony Event**	10b
K	Dingbat*	9
L	Stan's Plan, Left*	11b
M	Stan's Plan, Right*	10b
N	Suicide Lane*	10d
O	Juniper Junction	10a

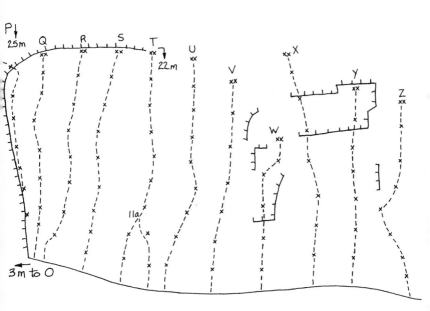

CORAL CRAG, RIGHT

P Katie's Korner** 8
Q Goodbye Mr Bond** 11c
R I'm a Little Teapot** 11d
S Lost in America** 11c
T Breakfast Surreal** 11a
U Hottentot Venus** 11c
V Throttler** 10d
W Stick-in-the-Mud* 10d
X Rocket Scientist** 11a
Y Never Forever* 10d
Z Nozzlehead* 10c

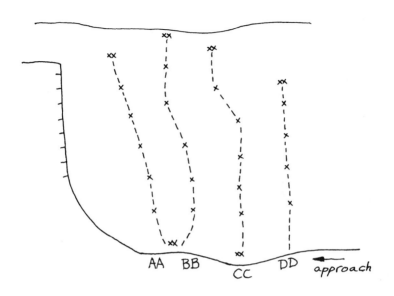

CORAL CRAG, UPPER RIGHT

AA	Techno-jumbo	10b
BB	Szechuan Chili	10b
CC	Jellobum	10d
DD	Grizzly Remains	10a

Ryno Van De Smit on Fear of the Hereafter (11c), Bataan (p. 172).
Photo Roger Chayer/TALUS Photographics.

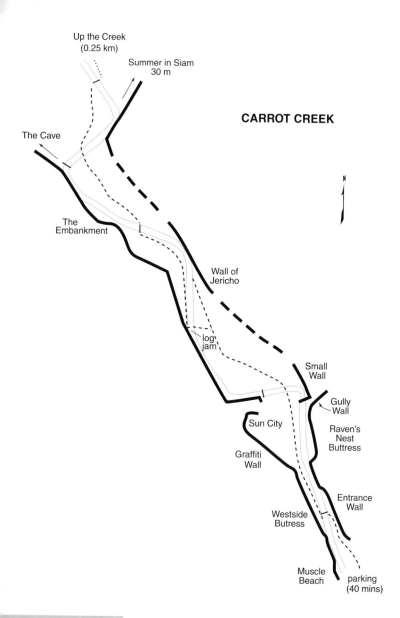

Up the Creek
(0.25 km)

Summer in Siam
30 m

CARROT CREEK

The Cave

The
Embankment

Wall of
Jericho

log
jam

Small
Wall

Gully
Wall

Sun City

Raven's
Nest
Buttress

Graffiti
Wall

Entrance
Wall

Westside
Butress

Muscle
Beach

parking
(40 mins)

N

> **The Fairholme Range Environmentally Sensitive Site**
> The climbing area and approach lie within The Fairholme Range ESS. The ESS designation does not mean that this is a legally closed area. However, overnight camping and cycling are prohibited and Parks Canada asks that climbers limit their use of this area. An information sign at the trailhead requests co-operation "in not entering this environmentally sensitive area." This request is generally being respected and this once very popular climbing area now sees very little traffic.

Carrot Creek boasts one of the highest concentrations of routes in the 5.11 - 5.12 range on local limestone. The climbs are located in a gorge, approximately 4 km northeast of the Trans-Canada Highway. Because the main gorge is so deep and narrow, temperatures there tend to be cooler than at other venues covered in this guide. The sun rarely reaches the rock on Raven's Nest Buttress, The Gully Wall and Graffiti Wall and the frigid waters of Carrot Creek keep the air there cool, even on the hottest of days. However, Sun City and Up the Creek catch the sun from late morning until mid afternoon and Muscle Beach, Westside Buttress and The Embankment come into the sun in early afternoon, so it is possible to climb on these cliffs from early spring until late fall. The Entrance Wall and Small Wall get late afternoon and evening sun in summer. The sunniest crags at Carrot Creek are The Frying Pan and The Cave. The latter is a sun trap, making it possible to climb there even in winter (on warmer days!).

The climbs at Carrot Creek are consistently steep, often overhanging, and usually sustained and strenuous. In the main part of the gorge they are often smooth at the start due to water polishing. The recommended descent from all climbs is by rappel. Most can be descended in 25 m raps, but **extreme caution** is advised if attempting this from the top of Raven's Nest Buttress as the steepness of the cliff makes it difficult to swing in to some of the intermediate rap stations. It is best to use two ropes to rap from here. Alternatively, walk down the back side of the cliff to a saddle and then south (right) to the start of the canyon. Virtually all the climbs are totally bolt protected. Of those that are not, only *Problems With Guinness* is recommended, and this requires only a 3.5 Friend.

If you do decide to go climbing here, two unique aspects of the canyon deserve special mention. First, the narrow gorge is a wildlife migration corridor, so please, **DO NOT TAKE DOGS TO THE AREA.** Second, there is nowhere suitable to shit in the main part of the canyon. If you must, go **downstream** from the climbing area where there is more soil and the canyon is wider, and at least pack out or burn your toilet paper!

Approach

Turn right from the west-bound lane of the Trans-Canada Highway at an unsigned road, 100 m west of a sign giving radio frequencies for Park Information (1.6 km west of the Banff Park entrance). Hop over or crawl under the fence near the far left corner of the parking area and follow a good trail (the first part of which is now partially blocked by felled trees to discourage use) through attractive open woodland to the gorge (40 minutes). There are no formal bridges and it may be necessary to ford the creek. On leaving the car park after climbing you **must** turn right (west); there is a break in the centre divide 1.3 km farther west where you can U-turn to drive east.

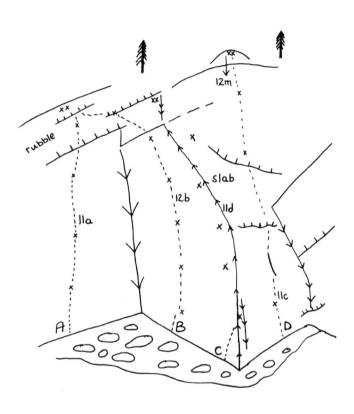

MUSCLE BEACH

A	Hard Bodies*	11a
B	The Venice Strut*	12b
C	Muscle Beach**	11d
D	Beach Balls	11c 0.5, 3.5 Friend (not recommended)

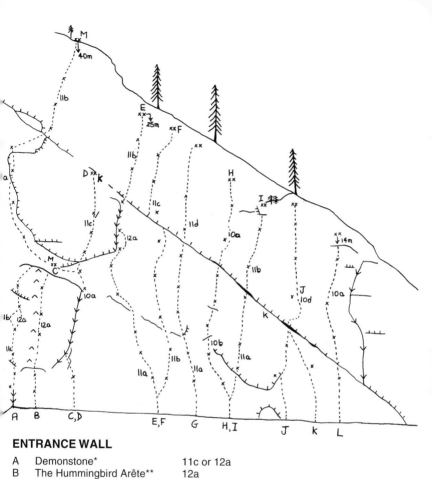

ENTRANCE WALL

A	Demonstone*	11c or 12a	
B	The Hummingbird Arête**	12a	
C	Book Worm	10a	nuts, 3.5 Friend
D	Higher Learning**	11c	
E	Open Book Exam**	12a	
F	Why Shoot the Teacher?**	11c	
G	Learning the Game*	11d	
H	Educational Process*	10b	
I	Quantum Physics*	11b	
J	Midterm*	10d	
L	Entrance Exam*	10a	
K	The Accidental Tourist	11a	TCUs, med. Friend (not recommended)
M	Advanced Education*	11b	

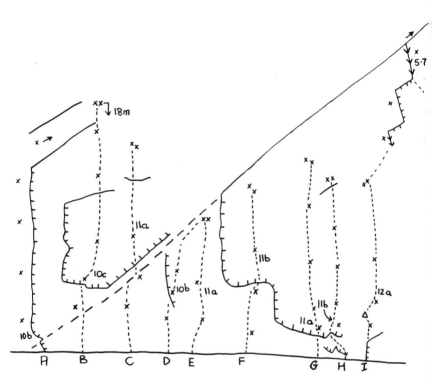

WESTSIDE BUTTRESS

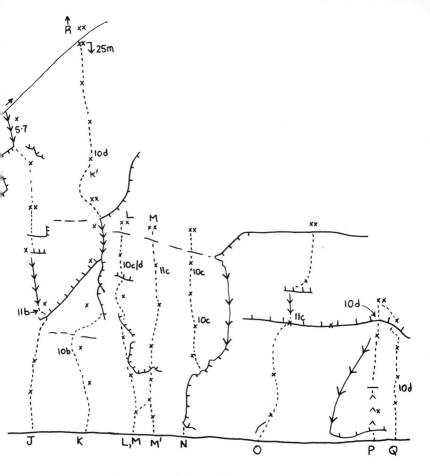

WESTSIDE BUTTRESS

J	Comfortably Numb**	11b	
K	Summertime Blues (P1)**	10b	
	Summertime Blues (P2)*	10d	
L	Bite the Rainbow**	10c/d	
M	Mistral (M' = tall person's start)*	11c	
N	Scirocco**	10c	
O	The Hardest 5.8 In the Rockies**	11c	
P	Aquacide*	10d	
Q	Monkey Puzzle	10d	
R	Silver Surfer**	12a	4 QDs

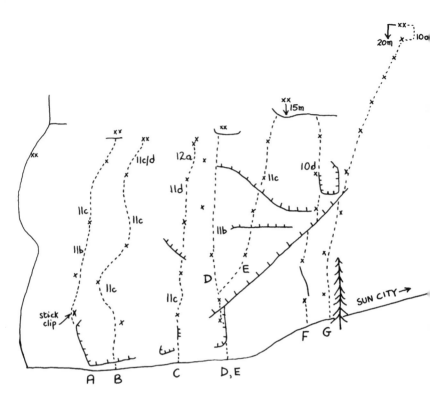

GRAFFITI WALL

A Dayglo Rage**   11c
B Physical Graffiti**   11d
C No More Mr Nice Guy**   12a
D Young Guns**   11b
E Suspended Sentence**   11c
F The Last Word*   10d
G American Graffiti*   10a

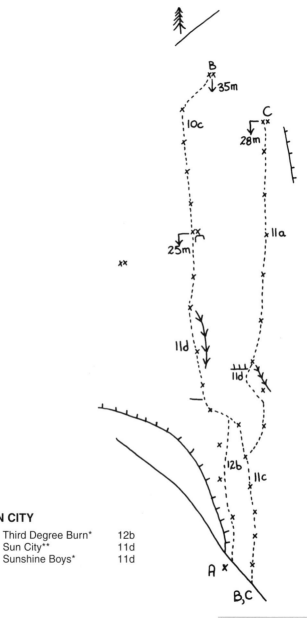

SUN CITY

A	Third Degree Burn*	12b
B	Sun City**	11d
C	Sunshine Boys*	11d

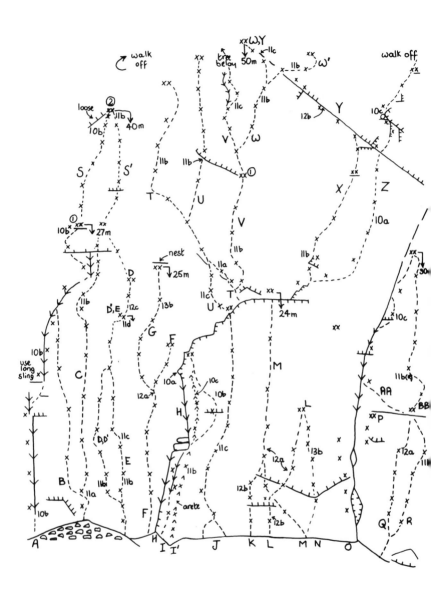

walk off

loose
② xx
10b' 11b
40m

S   S'

① xx
10b' 27m

D
11b
D,E 12c
11d
G   F
C
10a   10c
12a   10b
H
D,D' 11c
E
B 11b' 11b
11a
F arete
A H I I'

walk off
xx ω,Y
50m 11c
11b   ω'

tree
belay
11c   11b
V   ω
11b
11b ①
T   U
V
11b
11a
11c
U T
24m
nest
xx 25m
xx
M
L
12a 13b
12b
J K L M N

10c
Y
12b
X   Z
10a

ⓧ30
Z
10c

11b(c)
AA
xx BB
xxP
12a
Q R
O

RAVEN'S NEST BUTTRESS

A	Merlin's Laugh (alt. start)**	10b	
B	Merlin's Laugh (original start)**	11a	
C	The Magus**	11b	
D	The Sword In the Stone*	12c	
D'	The Short Sword**	11d	
E	Caliburn**	12a	
F	The Warlock**	12a	
G	American Standard**	13b	
H	The Copromancer	10a	gear to 3.5"
I	Coprophobia*	10b	
I'	Sidekick*	11b	
J	The Sorcerer's Apprentice**	11c	
K	The Lizard*	12b	
L	The Gizzard**	12b	
M	The Wizard**	12a	
N	Cup o' Joe	13b	
O	project		
P	project		
Q	Shadow of a Thin Man**	12a	
R	110 In the Shade**	11b	
S	Merlin's Laugh (pitch 2)*	10b	
S'	The Magus (pitch 2)**	11b	
T	Witches Brew	11b	
U	The Illusionist**	11c	
V	Hocus Pocus*	11c	best done as 2 pitches
W	Stolen Thunder	11c	
W'	Stolen Thunder (alt. finish)	11b	
X	Prince of Darkness*	11b	
Y	Nothing Up My Sleeves**	12b	
Z	The Enchantress*	10c	
AA	Dirty Trick	10c	
BB	No Sloppy Seconds**	11bR	opt #6 Rock

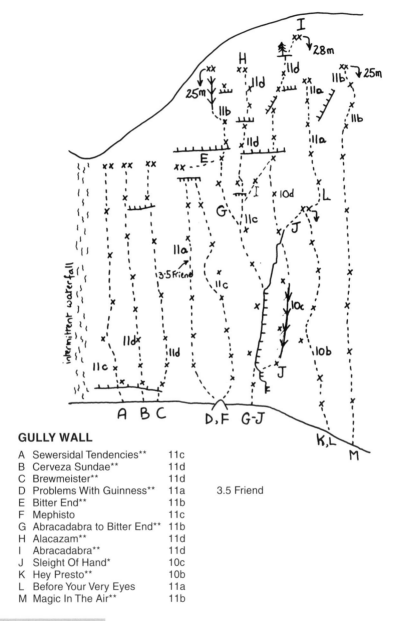

GULLY WALL

A	Sewersidal Tendencies**	11c
B	Cerveza Sundae**	11d
C	Brewmeister**	11d
D	Problems With Guinness**	11a
E	Bitter End**	11b
F	Mephisto	11c
G	Abracadabra to Bitter End**	11b
H	Alacazam**	11d
I	Abracadabra**	11d
J	Sleight Of Hand*	10c
K	Hey Presto**	10b
L	Before Your Very Eyes	11a
M	Magic In The Air**	11b

3.5 Friend

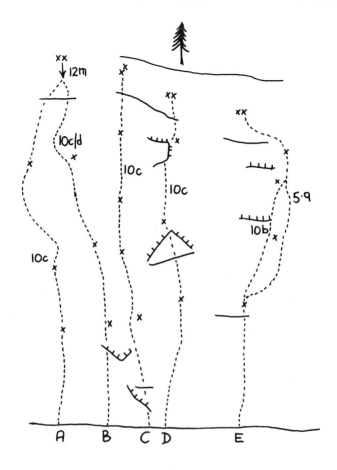

SMALL WALL

A	Small Fry	10c
B	Think Tall	10c/d
C	Vandals in Babylon*	10c
D	Small Is Beautiful**	10c
E	Grime and Punishment	9

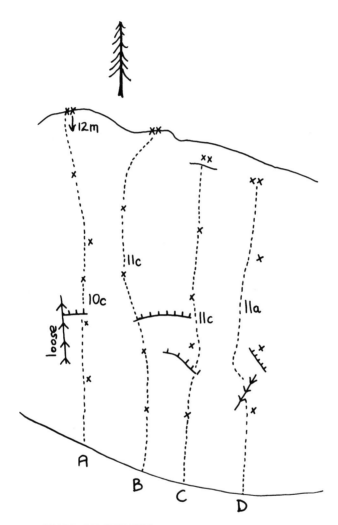

WALL OF JERICHO

A Equinox*   10c
B Fall Guy*   11c
C Silent Scream*   11c
D The Phoenix**   11a

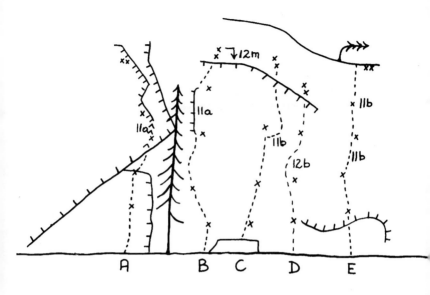

THE EMBANKMENT

JD LeBlanc on Doppio (13b),
Carrot Creek (p. 129). Photo Lev Pinter.

FRYING PAN

A Breakfast in America*   10c
B Have a Nice Day*   11b
C Toast**   12a
D Sunny Side Up**   11a
E Easy Over   10c

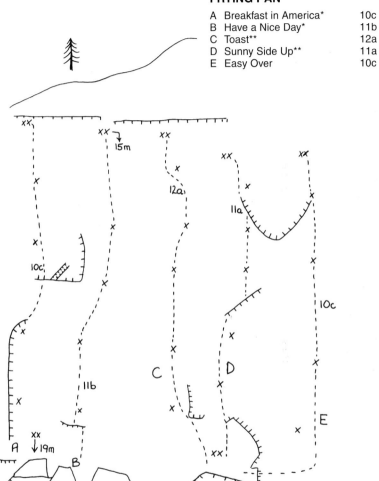

Frying Pan approach: 20 m downstream (left) of The Embankment is a ramp that diagonals up to the right. Follow this for 10 m and then climb back left at a bolt by a nose of rock (easy, but exposed). Continue easily up and left to the base of the wall.

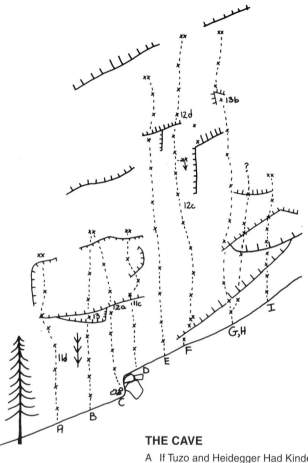

THE CAVE

A If Tuzo and Heidegger Had Kinder   11d
B Liar   13a
C Anti-Oedipus   12a
D The Allegory of My Sore Back   11c
E project
F Elmer Fudd   12d
G Mouthful of Freddie**   13b
H project

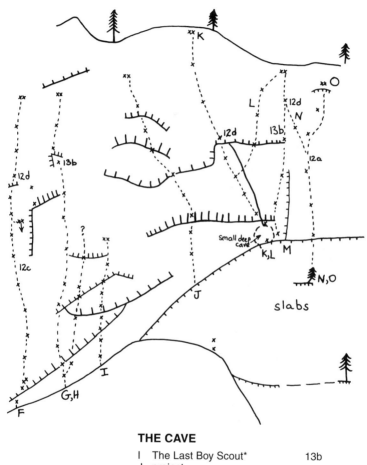

THE CAVE

I	The Last Boy Scout*	13b
J	project	
K	Carnivore	12d
L	project	
M	Doppio**	13b
N	Black Coffee**	12d
O	Gorilla Warfare**	12a

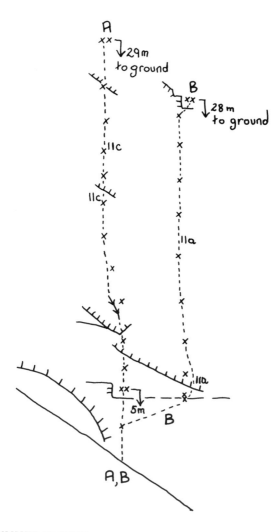

A
xx ↓29m
to ground

B
xx ↓28m
to ground

x

x 11c

x

11c x

x

x

x

11a

x

x

x

x 11a

xx ↓5m
B

x

A,B

SUMMER IN SIAM

A Summer in Siam**   11c
B Whistling in the Dark**   11a/b

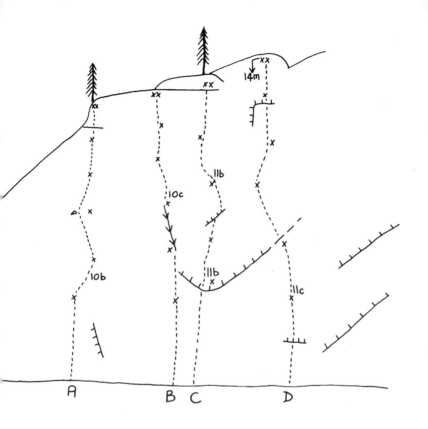

UP THE CREEK

A Up the Creek*   10b
B Away From It All**   10c
C Underhanded Tactics**   11b
D Feeling the Pinch*   11c

BATHTUB BROOK

This relatively undeveloped area is located in the drainage north of Harvie Heights (three drainages northwest of The Stoneworks). The climbs are on two cliffs: French Made Crag, a steep wall on the left (northwest) side of the creek; and Firé Wall, a steep slab across the creek from French Made Crag. All routes are fully equipped. The routes on Firé Wall have received very few ascents and so no quality ratings are given.

Approach
From the Harvie Heights access road, follow Rundle Road to its end and park at a locked gate. Continue up a gravel road (private land) to a quarry. Bypass the quarry on the right and continue up past a waterfall to gain the creek bed above. Follow the creek bed past some enjoyable slickrock scrambling, eventually reaching the cliffs in about 45 minutes from Harvie Heights. The approach is tricky except in dry weather when the creek is low.

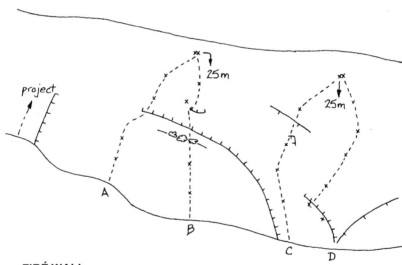

FIRÉ WALL

A	Firé Extinguisher	10b
B	Mickey Mantle	10a
C	Firé Alarm	11a
D	Smear Campaign	11c

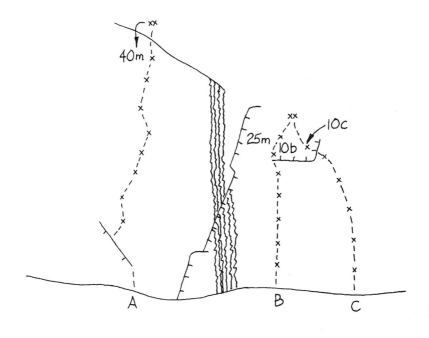

FRENCH MADE CRAG

A	French Made*	10b
B	Hotwire*	10b
C	Madame X*	10c

THE ALCOVE

This area is in a small, south-facing amphitheatre formed by a waterfall in the second drainage east of Bathtub Brook (the first major drainage west of The Stoneworks). The routes are equipped.

Approach

From the Harvie Heights access road, follow Rundle Road past some communications towers in a large clearing on the right. Park near a gated gravel road at the far end of the clearing. Walk up the gravel road to another clearing with a communication tower (about 8 minutes). Pick up a trail at the far left corner of the clearing and follow it for about 1 minute to a watercourse. Do not follow this drainage. Instead, follow the trail up the hill on the right to the top of a terrace. Walk east along the terrace for about 10 minutes to another watercourse and follow this up to The Alcove. Total approach time, about 35 minutes.

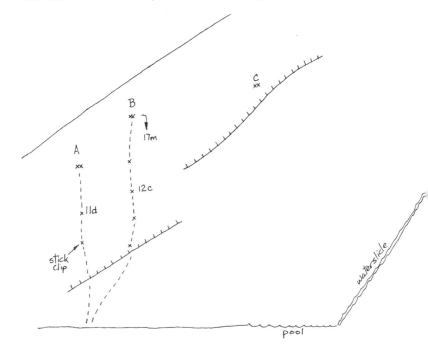

THE ALCOVE, LEFT SIDE

A The Interrogator*   11d
B Hold Your Own**   12c
C project

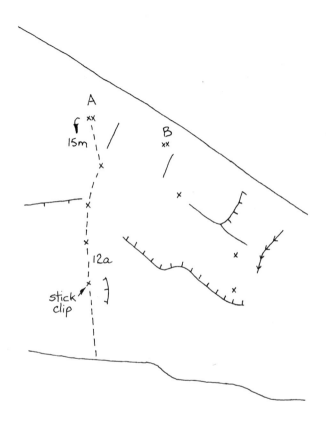

THE ALCOVE, RIGHT SIDE

A Hot Box**   12a
B project

THE STONEWORKS

This area is located in the drainage immediately left (northwest) of Mount Lady Macdonald. The main climbing area is a narrow, twisting, water-smoothed gorge called the Lower Canyon. Other routes are found on two cliffs a short distance beyond the end of this gorge: Weird Wall, a short, steep, south-facing cliff; and The Arcade, a large, north-facing wall set at a more moderate angle. All climbs except *Of Merging Ages* are fully equipped and all but *Basic Black* can be descended using one 50 m rope. Wait for warm weather to climb here—most of the routes see little or no sun.

Approach

From the Trans-Canada Highway, take the west Canmore exit and drive east along the service road that parallels the Trans-Canada on the north side. The service road can also be reached by turning west from Benchlands Trail, which crosses the Trans-Canada farther east at an overpass. Park at a gate approximately opposite the Shell station across the highway. The gate is at the crest of a hill, 1.3 km from the west Canmore exit and 2 km from Benchlands Trail. Cross the fence and walk up a short, steep paved road into a clearing. The drainage is ahead and slightly left. Follow trails and abandoned roads, reclosing any gates you go through, until the valley narrows and you are forced into the creek bed. It is possible to bicycle to this point. Continue up the creek bed to the canyon—a pleasant 45 minutes or so from the parking spot. To reach Weird Wall, walk up the creek bed a couple of minutes beyond the top end of the canyon until you reach a small cliff on the left, just a few metres above the valley bottom. This point also marks the start of the trail to The Arcade, which heads up right through boulders and scree to reach the cliff at *The Tempest*. **DO NOT ATTEMPT TO GET TO THE ARCADE DIRECTLY FROM THE HEAD OF THE CANYON BY FOLLOWING ALONG THE BASE OF THE CLIFFS.** This slope is readily eroded and is littered with large unstable boulders; furthermore, it doesn't save any time to go that way.

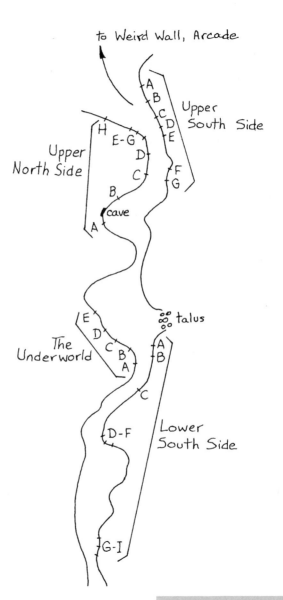

to Weird Wall, Arcade

A
B
C
D
E
Upper
South Side

F
G

Upper
North Side

H
E-G
D

C

B
cave

A

E
D
C B
A

The
Underworld

talus

A
B

C

Lower
South Side

D-F

G-I

The Stoneworks – 137

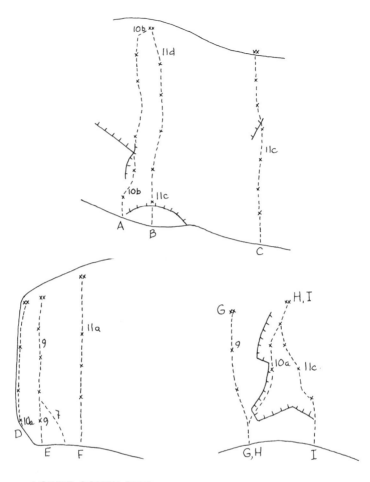

LOWER SOUTH SIDE

A So It's a Sport Climb**   10b
B Wings of Desire*   11d
C Spider in a Tub**   11c
D Kali*   10a
E Loki*   9
F Runners on 'Roids*   11a
G Girl Muscles*   9
H Clip Trip*   10a
I Power Hour**   11c

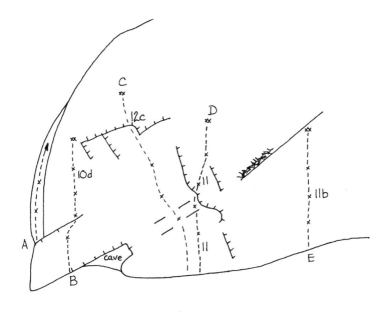

THE UNDERWORLD

A	Access Line	9
B	Wise Guys**	10d
C	Debauchery	12c R/X
D	Capone**	11b
E	Younger Than Yesterday*	11b

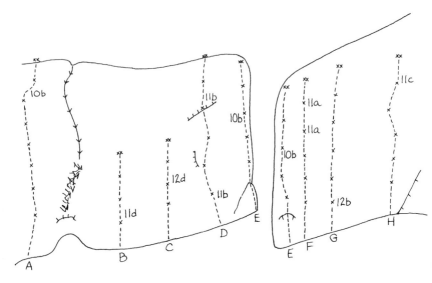

UPPER NORTH SIDE

A	Cro Magnon**	10b
B	Klingon War*	11c/d
C	Slap Shot	12d
D	Hat Trick**	11b
E	Penguin Lust**	10b
F	Electric Ocean**	11a
G	Blue Lotus*	12b
H	Love and Death	11c

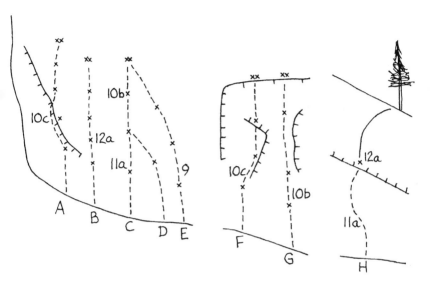

UPPER SOUTH SIDE

A Under the Gun**   10c
B Brent's Big Birthday* 12a/b
C Holey Redeemer Direct* 11a
D Holey Redeemer*   10b
E Baby Buoux*   9
F Junior Woodchuck Jamboree* 10c
G Boy Scout Fundraiser* 10b
H Of Merging Ages**   12aX Rock 2

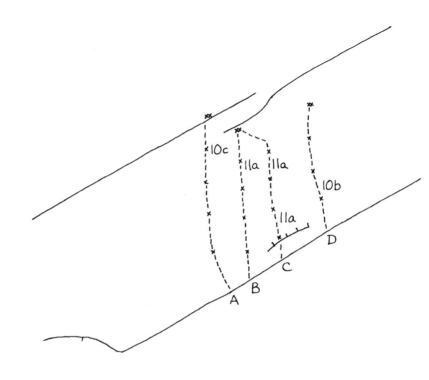

WEIRD WALL

A When the Going Gets Weird*   10c
B The Weird Turn Pro**   11a
C Gravity Rodeo**   11a/b
D Weird Noises*   10b

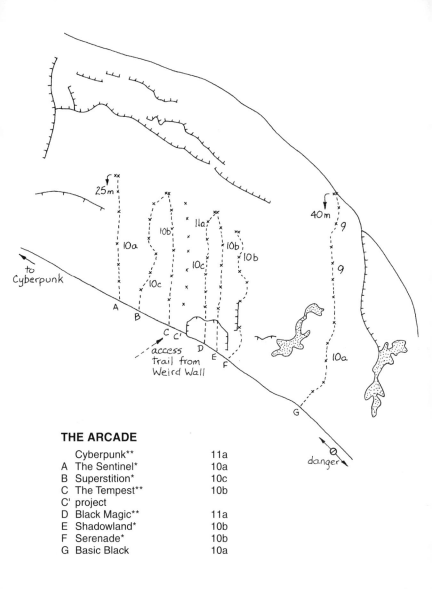

THE ARCADE

	Cyberpunk**	11a
A	The Sentinel*	10a
B	Superstition*	10c
C	The Tempest**	10b
C'	project	
D	Black Magic**	11a
E	Shadowland*	10b
F	Serenade*	10b
G	Basic Black	10a

COUGAR CANYON

Cougar Canyon is the prominent drainage immediately northeast of Canmore, between Mount Lady Macdonald and Grotto Mountain. All routes are fully equipped. As in all the canyons, chasing the sun becomes a major preoccupation on cool spring and fall days. The right side of House of Cards is the warmest morning crag in the canyon, catching full sun on even the shortest days. Other good morning areas are the upper end of Catseye Cliff, Catamount Crag, Cosmology Crag, Canadian Forks and Creekside Crag. Crowbar Crag gets afternoon sun; Chameleon Cliff and Made in the Shade come into the sun on summer evenings. Covert Crag and the south wall at Canadian Forks catch the sun nearly all day.

Approach
From the east: take Elk Run Boulevard, which leads north from Highway 1A about 500 m east of the Trans-Canada Highway interchange (the second entrance to Canmore on the east approach). After about 1 km, Elk Run Boulevard crosses Cougar Creek at the top of a gradual hill. From the west, or from Canmore, the same point is reached by taking Benchlands Trail, which crosses the Trans-Canada Highway by way of an overpass. Park in a lot west of the creek. Walk up a path and a road on the west side of the creek for about 1 km, then continue up a trail. There are several creek crossings but it is easy to keep your feet dry except when the water is high. Total walking time to the first climbing, at House of Cards Crag, is about 15 - 20 minutes; Cosmology Crag is about 15 minutes farther, and Creekside Crag is 20 - 25 minutes more.

Two climbs not pictured in this section have been done on cliffs about 15 minutes up the right (southeast) drainage from Canadian Forks. *Rage* (11b, 2 bolts) is at the left end of a short, very overhanging wall on the left side. The other bolts on this wall are projects. *Dark Eye of Sauron* (11c, 2 bolts) is on the other side of the drainage a short distance farther upstream.

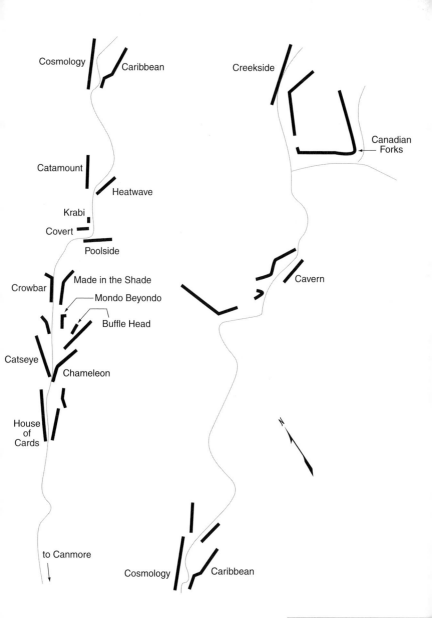

Cosmology

Caribbean

Creekside

Canadian
Forks

Catamount

Heatwave

Krabi

Covert

Poolside

Made in the Shade

Crowbar

Mondo Beyondo

Buffle Head

Cavern

Catseye

Chameleon

House
of
Cards

N

to Canmore

Cosmology

Caribbean

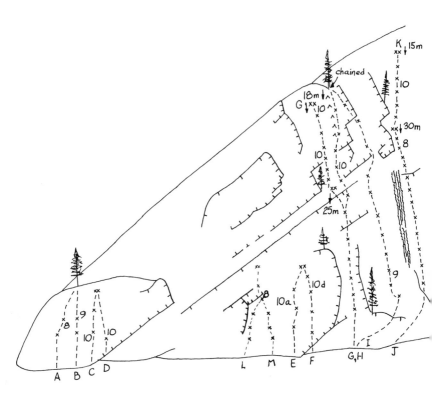

HOUSE OF CARDS, LEFT

A	Rock 201*	8
B	Empty Nest	9
C	Rock 301	10b
D	Rock 401*	10c
E	Innuendo	10a
F	Fly by Wire	10d
G	SPF*	10b
H	Solarium*	10a
I	Aqualung*	9
J	Slowpoke*	8
K	Fidget*	10c
L	Dreamcatcher in a Rusted Malibu	8
M	Kim and Murray	8

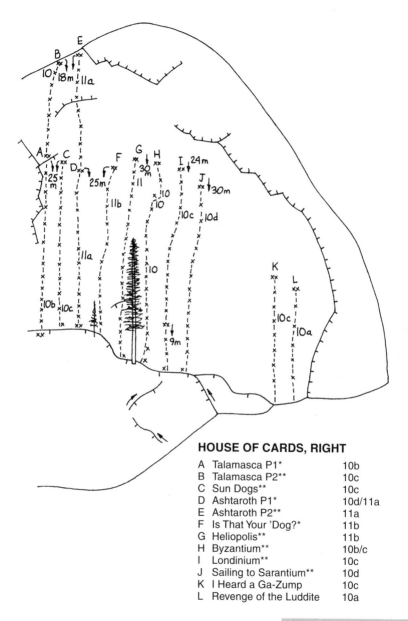

HOUSE OF CARDS, RIGHT

A	Talamasca P1*	10b
B	Talamasca P2**	10c
C	Sun Dogs**	10c
D	Ashtaroth P1*	10d/11a
E	Ashtaroth P2**	11a
F	Is That Your 'Dog?*	11b
G	Heliopolis**	11b
H	Byzantium**	10b/c
I	Londinium**	10c
J	Sailing to Sarantium**	10d
K	I Heard a Ga-Zump	10c
L	Revenge of the Luddite	10a

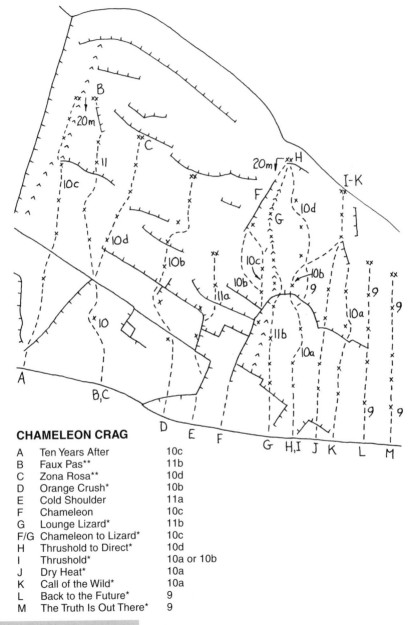

CHAMELEON CRAG

A	Ten Years After	10c
B	Faux Pas**	11b
C	Zona Rosa**	10d
D	Orange Crush*	10b
E	Cold Shoulder	11a
F	Chameleon	10c
G	Lounge Lizard*	11b
F/G	Chameleon to Lizard*	10c
H	Thrushold to Direct*	10d
I	Thrushold*	10a or 10b
J	Dry Heat*	10a
K	Call of the Wild*	10a
L	Back to the Future*	9
M	The Truth Is Out There*	9

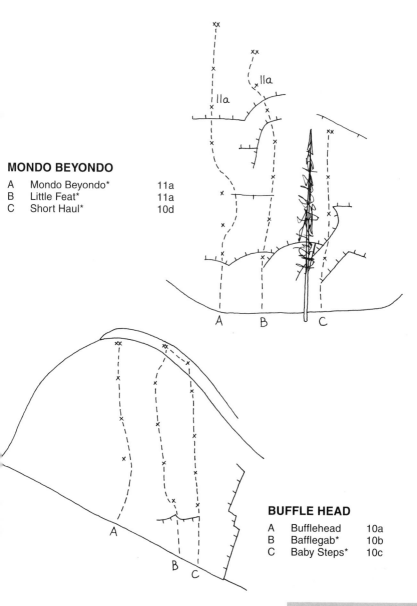

MONDO BEYONDO

A   Mondo Beyondo*   11a
B   Little Feat*   11a
C   Short Haul*   10d

BUFFLE HEAD

A   Bufflehead   10a
B   Bafflegab*   10b
C   Baby Steps*   10c

CATSEYE CLIFF, LEFT

A	Catspaw*	9+
A'	Catspaw Direct	10a
B	Catseye*	10b
C	Dr Tongue's 3D House of Slave Chicks*	11c
D	Double Header**	10a
D'	Double Play*	10d
E	Coconut Joe	11a/b
F	Banana Republic**	10a
F'	Banana Republic alt. start	
G	Ephemera*	11b
H	Iguana Moon Trek*	10a or 10c
I	Rough Trade*	11b
J	Virtual Light*	10a
K	Lapidarist	10c
L	Impulse	10a
M	Swan Lake	9+
N	Dressed to Kill**	11a/b
O	Incantation**	11c

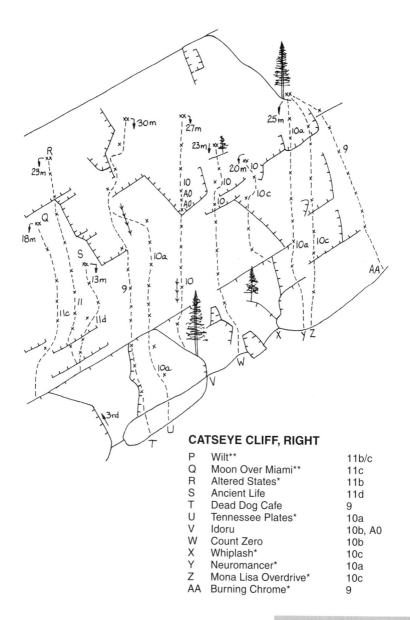

CATSEYE CLIFF, RIGHT

P	Wilt**	11b/c
Q	Moon Over Miami**	11c
R	Altered States*	11b
S	Ancient Life	11d
T	Dead Dog Cafe	9
U	Tennessee Plates*	10a
V	Idoru	10b, A0
W	Count Zero	10b
X	Whiplash*	10c
Y	Neuromancer*	10a
Z	Mona Lisa Overdrive*	10c
AA	Burning Chrome*	9

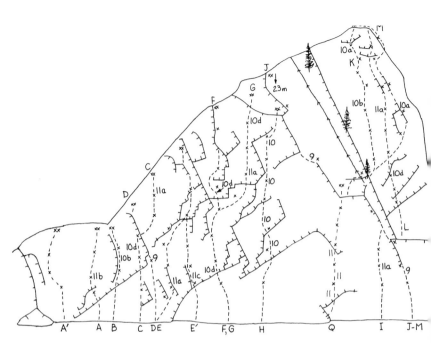

CROWBAR CRAG, LEFT (SOUTHEAST FACE)

A	Depth Charge	11b
A'	Lougheed the Great	7
B	Diptheria	10b
C	Terminal Velocity*	11a
D	Blockhead	9
E	Block Buster*	11a
E'	Doppler Effect**	11c
F	Shockwave**	10d
G	Surface Tension**	11a/b
H	Critical Mass**	10c
I	Island Experience*	11a
J	Islands in the Stream*	9
K	Face Value**	10b
L	Mean Street*	11a
M	Argon*	10a
Q	Suzie Q**	11c

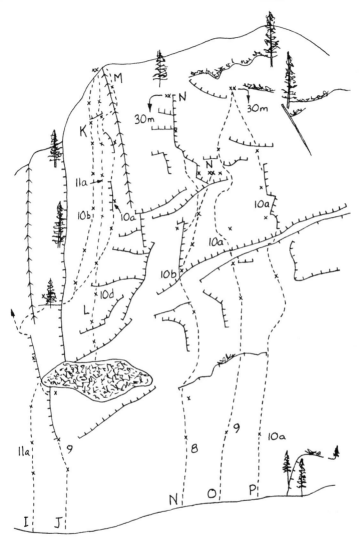

CROWBAR CRAG, RIGHT (NORTHEAST FACE)

L Mean Street*   11a
M Argon*   10a
N Jack of Clubs*   10b
O Sleeping Dog*   10a
P Slow Turning*   10a

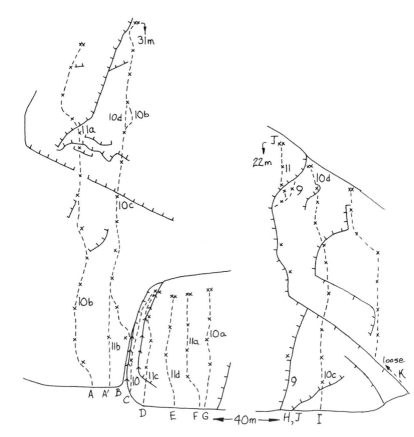

MADE IN THE SHADE

A	Tender Mercies*	11a	
A'	Shady Lady*	11b	stick clip
B	Made in the Shade**	10b/c	
C	Crashcourse	10b	stick clip
D	Clipjoint*	11c	stick clip
E	French Connection*	11d	stick clip
F	Tree Men**	11a	
G	Crybaby*	10a	
H	Shadow of Turning**	9	
I	High Wire**	10d	
J	Skyjack*	11b	
K	Pin-toe Flakes	10b/c	

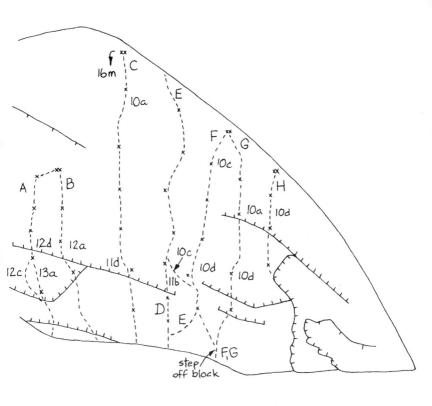

POOLSIDE CRAG

A	Stygian Ayre**	12d or 13a
B	Chandelle*	12a
C	Dark Star**	11d
D	Bob's Direct**	11b
E	Bob's Yer Uncle**	10c
F	Party Line**	10d
G	Poolside Pleasures**	10d
H	The Diving Board**	10d

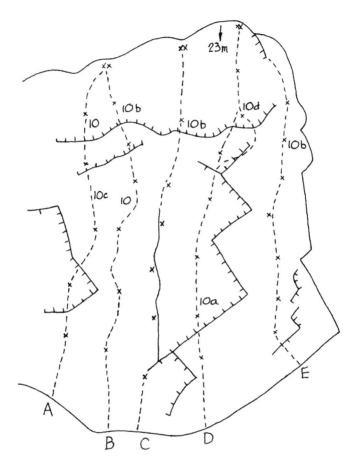

COVERT CRAG

A Cloak and Dagger*   10c
B Under Cover**   10b
C Covert Action*   10b
D Cover-up*   10d
E Deep Cover*   10b

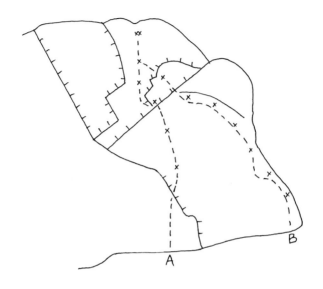

KRABI CRAG

A Ray of Thailand   10a/b
B Red Shirt in the Thai   11a/b

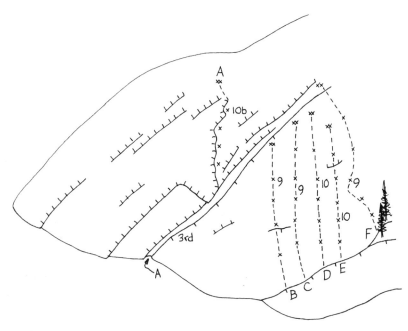

CATAMOUNT CRAG

A	Law and Order*	10b
B	Open Season*	9
C	Abilene**	9
D	Cabin Fever**	10b
E	Catamount	10a
F	Chisum Trail	9

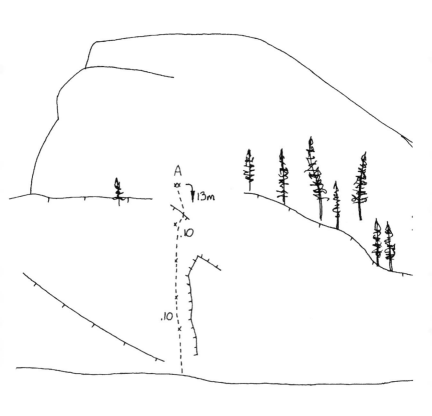

HEATWAVE

A   Heatwave   10c

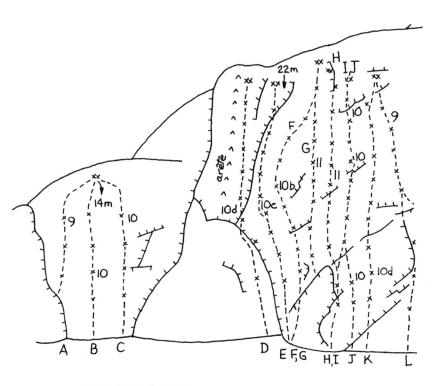

COSMOLOGY CRAG

A	Navigator	9
B	Nine to Five*	10b
C	Cat and Mouse*	10c
D	Archaos*	10d
E	Honeymoon Suite**	10c
F	Big Bang Theory**	10b
G	Event Horizon**	11a
H	Neutronium**	11a
I	Redshift*	10b
J	Indigo	10d
K	Lucille*	10d

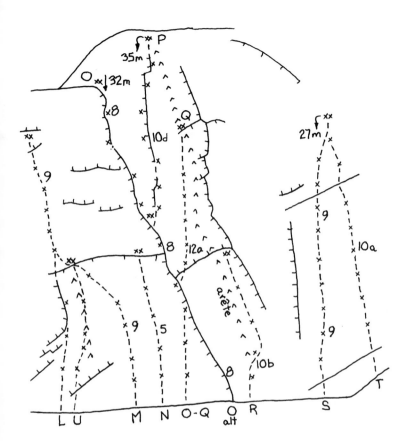

COSMOLOGY CRAG

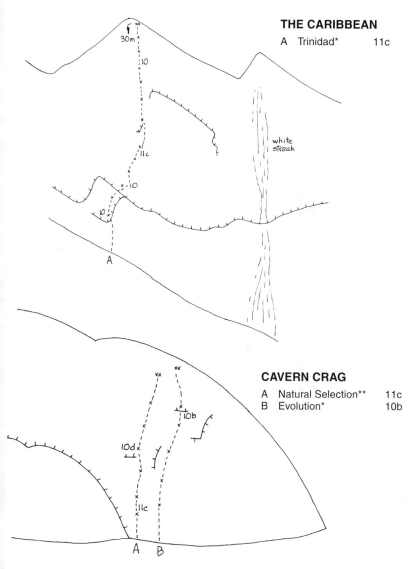

THE CARIBBEAN

A   Trinidad*   11c

30m
10
white
streak
11c
10
10
A

CAVERN CRAG

A   Natural Selection**   11c
B   Evolution*   10b

10b
10d
11c
A   B

*Pam Pearson on Poolside Pleasures (10d), Cougar Canyon (P. 155)
Photo Roger Chayer/TALUS Photographics.*

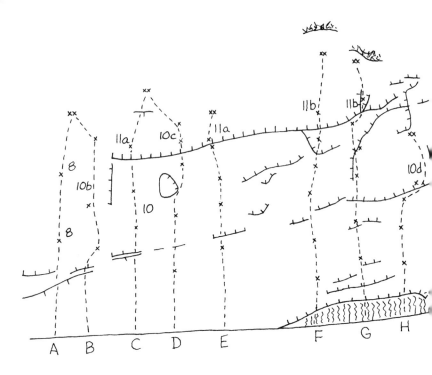

CREEKSIDE CRAG

A Hockey Night in Canada*   8
B Strandline*   10b
C Dynosoar*   11a/b
D Stone Cold*   10c
E Some Like It Hot*   11a
F Tilt*   11b
G Withering Heights**   11b
H Arcana**   10d

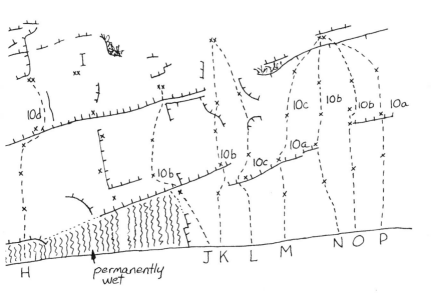

CREEKSIDE CRAG

I project
J Lunch Rambo Style*   10b
K Cafe Rambo*   10b
L Lysdexia**   10c
M When Worlds Collide*   10c
N Gondwanaland*   10b
O Continental Drift*   10b
P Burmese*   9/10a

LA PLAYA NEGRA

A The Nomadic Struggle   10d
B Prisoners of the Sun   10a

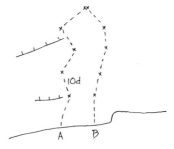

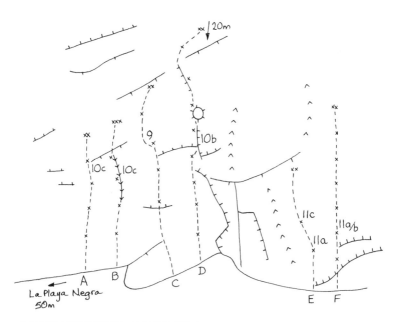

CANADIAN FORKS, SOUTHSIDE

A Prima Donna**   10c/d
B Diva**   10c/d
C Broken Chord   9
D Stepping Razor*   10b
E Danse Macabre*   11c
F Spite**   11a/b

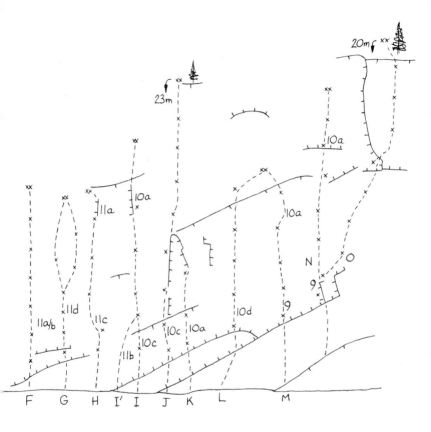

CANADIAN FORKS, EASTSIDE

F	Spite**	11a/b	
G	Elixir**	11d	
H	Phlogiston**	11c	
I	Free Lunch**	10c/d	
I'	Lean Cuisine	11b	toprope
J	Some Can Whistle*	10c	
K	Whistlestop**	10a	
L	Some Can Dance*	10d	
M	Carioca	10a	
N	Hidden Agenda	10a	
O	Ricochet*	9	

Great climbing on steep, high quality and in places densely pocketed limestone in an area with low snowfall and abundant sunshine. Sound too good to be true? Well, there is just one catch—a steep, 1 - 1.5 hour approach with an elevation gain of 800 metres! The area is named after the infamous Bataan Death March and although no one has actually died on the walk up to the crag, one climber did suffer a minor heart attack there a few years ago. However, more and more climbers and route-builders are deciding that the long slog up there is worth it. The potential for routes, particularly those in the 5.12 – 5.13 range, is, like the approach, staggering. A few of the routes here are equipped with (large) Metolius rap hangers to facilitate A0 moves that replace a move or two that are greatly out of context with the rest of the climb.

The rock faces southeast and southwest, so it catches maximum sunshine while at the same time remaining sheltered from the prevailing westerly winds. Bataan has the longest season of any area in the Bow Corridor, extending some years from late February until late October (although all but salamanders may find it too hot during midsummer). Bring lots of water, as there is *none* at the crag or on the approach. A 60 m rope is almost mandatory as many of the pitches are a *full* 30 m. You may find a ski or hiking pole useful, especially on the way down from the crag.

Please help to minimize soil erosion by sticking to the established trail, *especially* on your descent.

Approach

Bataan sits high on Grotto Mountain, a few kilometres east of Canmore and is located above the left (west) end of the prominent quarry scar that runs along the foot of the mountain. From Canmore, follow Highway 1A east towards Seebe. Go under the Highway 1 overpass to the Banff exit. From Calgary, take the first Canmore exit from Highway 1 after crossing the Bow River (signed Canmore and Highway 1A) to reach this point. Continue east on Highway 1A for another 2.3 km and park in an old gravel pit on the left (north) side of the road. (1 km west of the Burnco gravel pit if approaching from Seebe on Highway 1A.)

Climb steeply up the bank near the southeast corner of the gravel pit and find a faint trail that starts behind a tall solitary tree and skirts the edge of the excavation. Follow this up to a power line that runs along the bench. Cross under the power line and then turn left on the well-used horse trail that runs along the bench. After about 75 m, branch right onto a smaller trail where the horse trail crosses a dip (look for a cairn and flagging). Continue through fairly open woodland (flagged), crossing several game-trails which contour the slope, until you reach a large sparsely treed bench and a prominent forked tree beside a junction in the trail (10 - 15 minutes from parking). Cut back *right* and up (cairns) and head towards the left end of the quarry. Walk round the left edge of the quarry clearing to a well-flagged trail that starts in its top left corner (20 minutes from parking). Follow this as it zigzags steeply up the hillside to the bottom end of a long, easterly facing cliff which runs down the fall-line of the slope (50 – 60 minutes from parking). Continue for another 5 minutes via switchbacks up a steep, rubbly slope to a large rotten cave (The First Cave); the first climbs are located just to the left of the cave. The trail above climbs steeply, switchbacks into the trees a couple of times and then rejoins the crag at the area known as The Sweet Hereafter (10 minutes from The First Cave). Just right of this is a very prominent open book (The Dirty Book). The access trail continues up to the right and after a long switchback arrives at The Slab, near the start of *Crushed Velvet* (5 minutes from The Sweet Hereafter). Uphill from here the trail more or less parallels the base of an unbroken band of cliffs (refer to the location map below for locations of the individual climbing areas). After about 10 minutes, the cliff band

G Gravel Pit (parking),   SH Sweet Hereafter,   EB Eyes of Bataan,   T Tipperary,
FC First Cave,   FE Far East

curves round through a 90-degree angle to face southwest. Here two prominent caves mark The Eyes of Bataan. To their right is an impressive striped wall, The Pacific Theatre, which is bounded on its right by a rubbly chimney/gully system known as The Mountaineers' Route. Right of here the trail is flat and soon brings you to Tipperary and then The Far East (about 20 minutes from The Sweet Hereafter and 1.5 - 2 hours from parking).

Note: there is a hazard from rocks dislodged by sheep walking along scree ledges and the top of the crags *especially* in the vicinity of Tipperary.

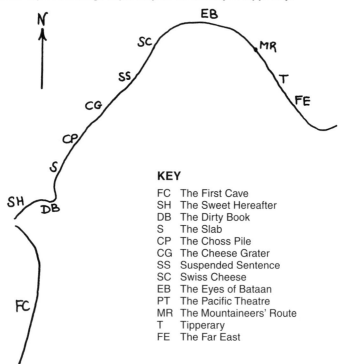

KEY

FC   The First Cave
SH   The Sweet Hereafter
DB   The Dirty Book
S   The Slab
CP   The Choss Pile
CG   The Cheese Grater
SS   Suspended Sentence
SC   Swiss Cheese
EB   The Eyes of Bataan
PT   The Pacific Theatre
MR The Mountaineers' Route
T   Tipperary
FE   The Far East

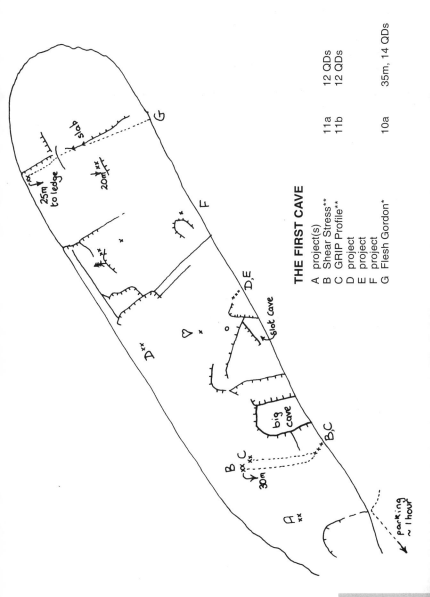

THE FIRST CAVE

A project(s)
B Shear Stress**   11a   12 QDs
C GRIP Profile**   11b   12 QDs
D project
E project
F project
G Flesh Gordon*   10a   35m, 14 QDs

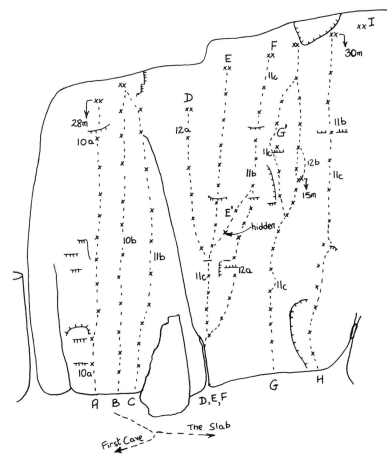

THE SWEET HEREAFTER

A	Fingers in a Blender**	10a
B	Jaws**	10b
C	Fresco*	11b/c
D	Too Little, Too Late*	12a
E	Culture of Fear*	12a
E'	Fear of the Hereafter**	11c
F	The Sweet Hereafter**	12a
G	With or Without You**	12b
G'	Faraway, So Close**	11c/d
H	The Filth and the Fury**	11c/d
I	project	

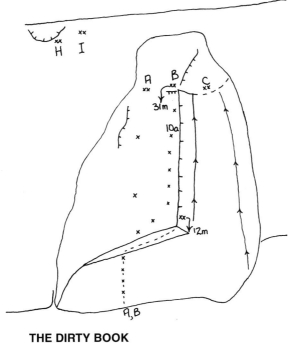

THE DIRTY BOOK

A   project
B   Dirty Book*   10a   35m
C   project

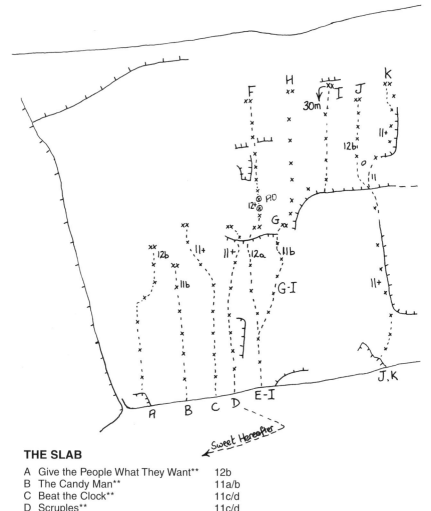

THE SLAB

A Give the People What They Want**   12b
B The Candy Man**   11a/b
C Beat the Clock**   11c/d
D Scruples**   11c/d
E Crushed Velvet P1**   12a
F Crushed Velvet P2**   12d or 12a A0
G Exit Planet Dust**   11b
H project
I The Arch**   12d
J Heavy Breathing**   12b
K Crank Call**   11d

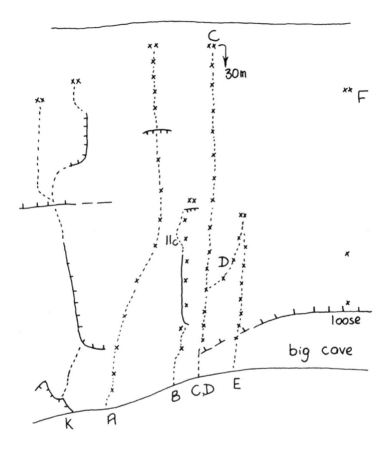

THE CHOSS PILE

A	September Eleven**	12c
B	Buena Vista Social Club**	11c
C	The Way of All Flesh**	12b
D	Post Apocalyptic Wasteland**	12a/b
E	Jive Turkey Direct*	12c
F	open project	

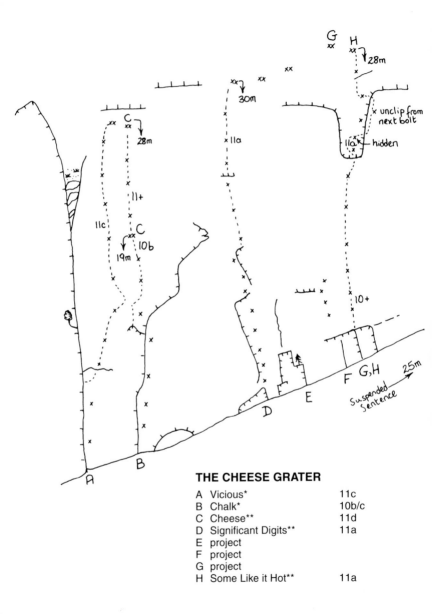

THE CHEESE GRATER

A Vicious*   11c
B Chalk*   10b/c
C Cheese**   11d
D Significant Digits** 11a
E project
F project
G project
H Some Like it Hot**   11a

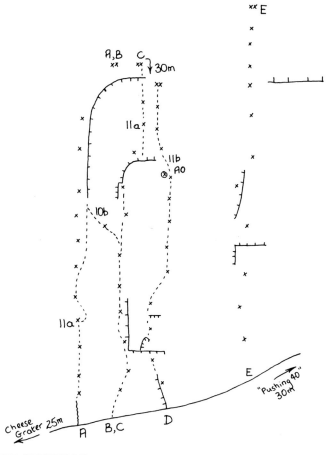

SUSPENDED SENTENCE

A Broken English*   11a
B Suspended Sentence**   10b
C Dangling Modifier**   11a
D Ghosts of Thousands   11b A0
E open project

30 m uphill from here, just before the cliff starts to curve round to the east, is a prominent overhanging corner crack/groove *Pushing 40*** (37 m, 11b/c, 16 clips). This is best climbed using a 70 m rope, but you can mange with a 60 m by back-clipping to a lower-off rap ring at about one third height.

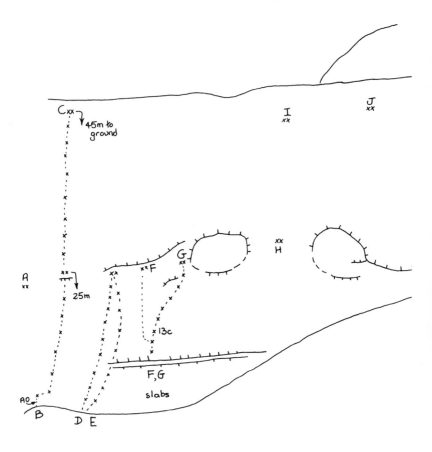

THE EYES OF BATAAN

A	open project	
B	Nirvana**	12d/13a A0 or 13c
C	Truckasaurus**	12a
D	24 Frames per Second**	13a/b
E	project	
F	open project	
G	Jacob's Ladder**	13c
H-I	open projects	

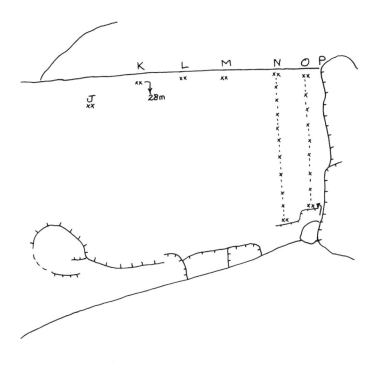

THE PACIFIC THEATRE

J-M open projects
N   Cartoon**   12d
O   Dressed up in Pearls**   12a
P   Mountaineers' Route   easy 5th class loose, dangerous

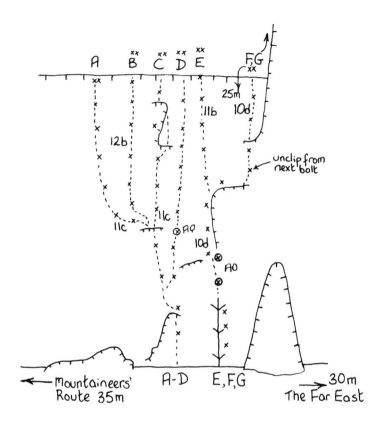

BATAAN, TIPPERARY

A	Saving Grace**	11c	
B	It's a Long Long Way*	12b	
C	Thief**	11c	
D	Burning Desire**	12a A0	
E	Tipperary**	11b A0 or 11d	
F	Far Corner of the Earth P1**	10d A0 or 11d	
G	Far Corner of the Earth P2**	10c	7 QDs

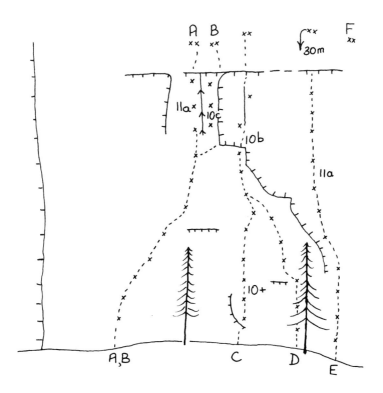

THE FAR EAST

A Mutton Chops**   11a
B Mutton Chops alt. finish*   10c
C Jagged Edge*   10d
D Jagged Edge, alt. start*   10b
E Death by a Thousand Cuts*   11a
F project

Originally known for its multi-pitch climbs on appalling rock, Crag X now has good quality sport climbs at its left end. The southerly aspect and short approach (10 minutes) make it possible to climb here even in winter (on warm days). Be warned that the slopes around Crag X are heavily infested with wood ticks in spring.

Approach

Park on the shoulder of Highway 1A near the Grotto Creek Pit road, 1.7 km west of the Baymag #2 Plant turn-off and 300 m east of Gap Lake picnic area. The road leads to a gravel pit owned by Lafarge and is signed "no trespassing," but it is OK to walk on it. Go down the road for about 250 m to a rough trail flagged with yellow tape that starts on the left, just before the aptly named "Howling Dog Kennels." Follow the trail around the northern perimeter of the kennel fence. Continue for another 75 m to a large broken tree. Here a faint trail splits off left and leads directly up the hillside to the base of the crag. *Sideline* is the prominent corner above a large toppled tree about 40 m east (right) of the top of the approach trail.

CRAG X

A	X-terminator**	10c	
B	Sideline**	9	gear to 2"
B'	Sideline Variations		gear to 2"
C	Double Cross*	10c	
C'	Double Cross Direct*	12a	
D	Mainline*	10c	
E	Mr Clean	11b/c	
F	Saigon Kiss**	11d	
G	Bombs Away*	11c	nuts, Friend 2.5, small TCU
H	Bandits at 2 O'Clock**	11b	
I	Pilot Error*	10c	gear to Friend 3
J	Both Guns Blazing*	11d	wired nuts, RP 3

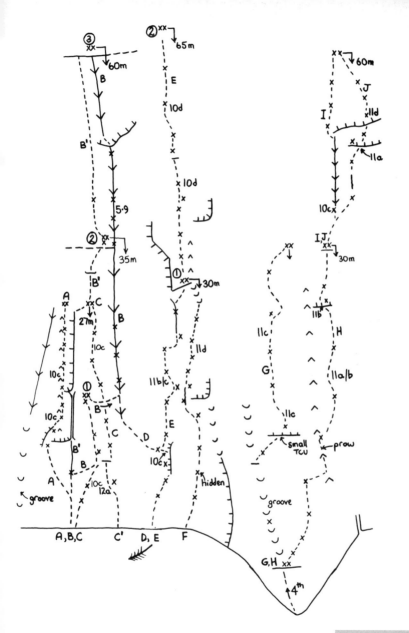

Crag X – 183

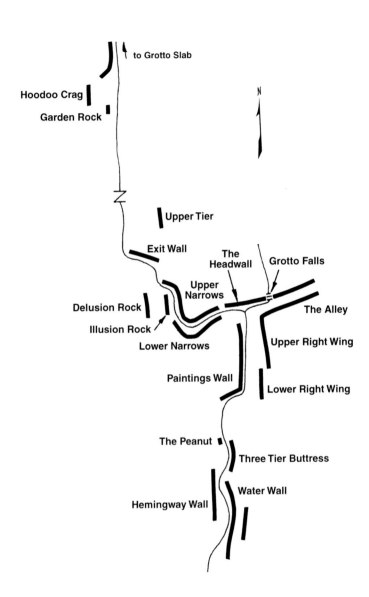

to Grotto Slab

N

Hoodoo Crag
Garden Rock

Upper Tier

Exit Wall

The Headwall   Grotto Falls

Upper Narrows

Delusion Rock

The Alley

Illusion Rock

Upper Right Wing

Lower Narrows

Paintings Wall

Lower Right Wing

The Peanut

Three Tier Buttress

Water Wall

Hemingway Wall

GROTTO CANYON

Grotto Canyon is located in the deep valley immediately east of Grotto Mountain. Many of the climbs are modern sport routes, but some were established from the ground up and others date from the early days of rap bolting, when protection was often sketchy by today's standards. Despite a fair bit of retrofitting, some of the climbs still have loose rock, are poorly protected (especially near the ground), and/or lack proper top anchors. Rock polishing has occurred on several cliffs, Illusion Rock being the most badly affected. The routes here have become slippery and dangerous to lead as a result of excessive toproping. Sunshine is often hard to find in Grotto Canyon, and several of the cliffs languish in perpetual shade. In the main canyon, Hemingway Wall is the only climbing area that catches morning sun; Water Wall Right, Paintings Wall South, the Upper Right Wing and the Upper Narrows are the sunniest places in the afternoon. The Alley catches late afternoon and evening sun. Farther upstream, Hoodoo Crag is warm in the morning and the Upper Tier and Grotto Slab come into the sun in the afternoon. A few of the climbs in The Narrows and at Grotto Slab require two ropes, but one is enough everywhere else.

Approach

The recommended approach starts from a gravel parking lot north of Highway 1A, 4.5 km west of the gas station in Exshaw. If you are coming from the west, look for the parking lot partway around the first bend to the left after you pass Gap Lake and Crag X. A narrow trail starts through the trees just left (west) of the Baymag #2 Plant. Cross a rail line and follow the trail to a powerline right of way. Continue north over a grassy knoll (the Baymag water supply reservoir) a short distance to the canyon mouth. From this point the main "trail" follows the stream bed, crossing the creek numerous times. The first four creek crossings can be avoided by taking a trail through the trees on the right (east) bank. This trail is used to reach The Uncharted Sea, a blackish slab of rock (visible from the road) on the east side of Grotto Creek Valley, above The Alley. Look for a pale slab of rock a short distance up on the right, just before you get to the first major right bend in the valley. Find a marked trail at this slab and follow it first up the hill, then left, for about 30 minutes to The Uncharted Sea (p. 213).

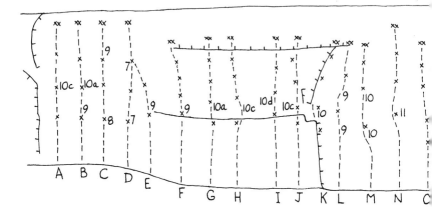

WATER WALL, LEFT

A	Raindust	10c
B	Soft Option*	10a/b
C	Kinesthesia*	9
D	Breezin'*	7
E	Ill Wind	9
F	Canary in a Coal Mine	9
G	Deviant Behaviour	10a
H	Loose Lips Sink Ships	10c
I	Lip Service*	10d
J	Power Play*	10c
K	Spring Clean*	10a
L	Denkem*	10a
M	The Ablutor*	10c
N	Scarface	11b
O	For Whom the Bell Tolls*	11b

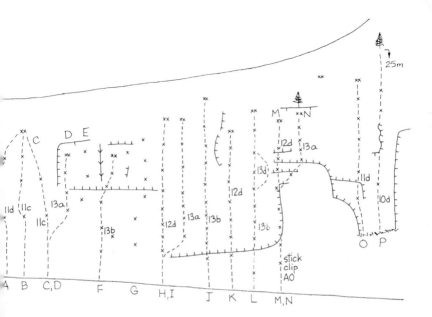

WATER WALL, RIGHT

A	Reflex Action	11d	
B	Cerebral Goretex	11c	
C	Across the River and into the Trees	11c	
D	Cause and Effect	13a/b	
E	project		
F	Burn Hollywood Burn	13b	drilled holds
G	project		
H	Shep's Diner	13a	drilled holds
I	Bloody Outsiders	13a	
J	The Resurrection	13b	drilled holds
K	Crimes of Passion	12d	drilled holds
L	Vapor Trails	13b or 13d	
M	Tintin and Snowy Get Psyched**	12d	
N	Metabolica**	13a	
O	Urban Youth	11d	
P	The Sting*	10d	

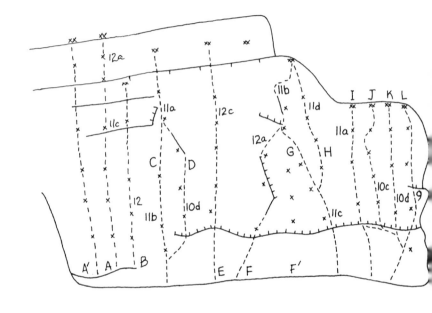

HEMINGWAY WALL, LEFT

A	The Importance of Being Ernest**	12a	
A'	Death in the Afternoon	12a	
B	Cracked Rhythm*	12b/c	
C	Chips Are for Kids**	11b	
D	Farewell to Arms**	11a	
E	Tropicana	12c	chipped holds
F	Success Pool**	12a	
F'	Unknown (project?)		
G	Walk on the Wilde Side**	11c	
H	Stone Age Romeos**	11d	
I	Grey Matter*	11a	
J	Grand Larceny*	10c/d	
K	Petty Theft*	10d	
L	Falling from Heaven*	9	

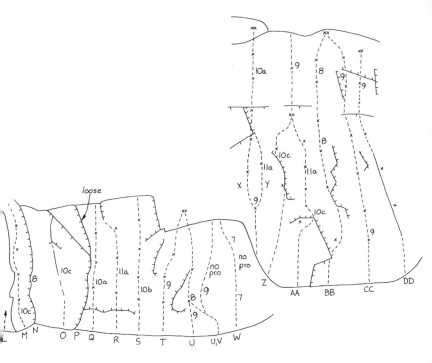

HEMINGWAY WALL, RIGHT

L	Falling from Heaven*	9	
M	Zipcode	10c	
N	Little Canadian Corner	8	gear to 3"
O	Lively Up Yourself	10c	gear to 2"
P	Flake Line	6	not recommended
Q	Runaway	10a	
R	Footloose	11aR	
S	Run of the River**	10b	
T	Walk the Line*	9	
U	Cakewalk*	8 or 9	
V	Oh No Not Another	9	
W	Yet Another	7	
X	Layla*	10a	
Y	Delilah*	11a	
Z	Temptress**	10c	
AA	Siren Song**	11a	
BB	Nymphet**	8	
CC	Scheherazade**	9	
DD	Lola*	9	

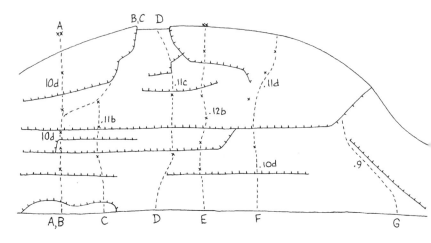

THREE TIER BUTTRESS

A	Stiff Upper Lip	10d
B	Short and Curly	10d
C	Too Low for Zero	11b
D	High Octane*	11c
E	Dr No*	12b
F	Mr Olympia*	11d
G	Rising Damp	9

THE PEANUT

A KP Special 11a

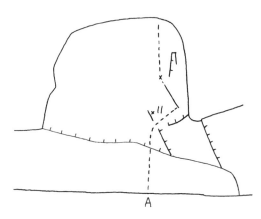

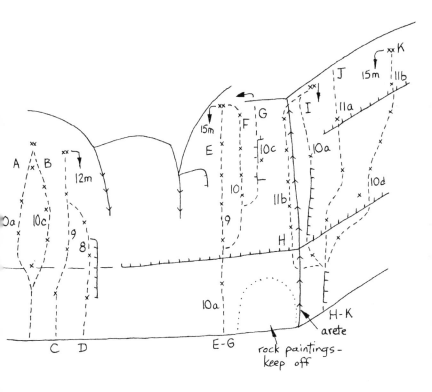

PAINTINGS WALL, SOUTH

A	Blaster*	10a
B	Blindside	10c
C	Scavenger*	9
D	OK Corral*	8
E	Art of the Ancients**	9
F	Retrospective**	10a/b
G	Left to Chance	10c
H	Cultural Imperative**	11b
I	Artful Dodger*	10a	gear to 1.5"
J	Peter Pan	11a
K	Sidewinder**	11b

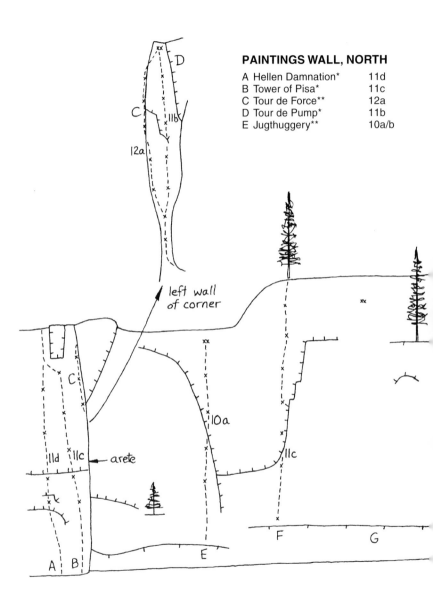

PAINTINGS WALL, NORTH

A Hellen Damnation*   11d
B Tower of Pisa*   11c
C Tour de Force**   12a
D Tour de Pump*   11b
E Jugthuggery**   10a/b

D

C   11b

12a

left wall
of corner

C

11d   11c   ← arete

10a

11c

A   B   E   F   G

PAINTINGS WALL, NORTH

F   Fly by Night*   11c
G   project
H   Fast Forward*   10c
I   Walk Don't Run*   11b
J   Rush*   11b
K   project
L   Layaway Plan*   10c
M   Watusi Wedding**   10a
N   Jesus Drives a Cadillac* 10b

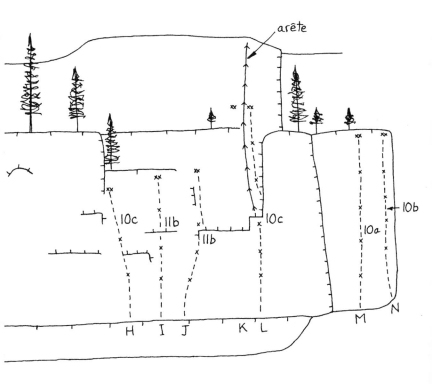

The **Lower Right Wing** is most conveniently reached by heading up and left along a trail that starts across the creek from *Art of the Ancients*, on Paintings Wall. Continue up and left to get to the **Upper Right Wing.** The Upper Right Wing is also readily accessible from the fork in the creek at the base of The Headwall.

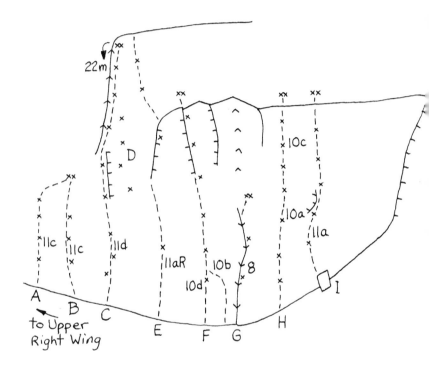

LOWER RIGHT WING

A	Soma*	11c	
B	Hush*	11c	
C	Subliminal Seduction*	11d	
D	project		
E	Lunatic Madness	11aR	not recommended
F	Lithium*	10b or 10d	
G	Joyride*	8	
H	Aggressive Treatment*	10c/d	
I	Night Life*	11a	

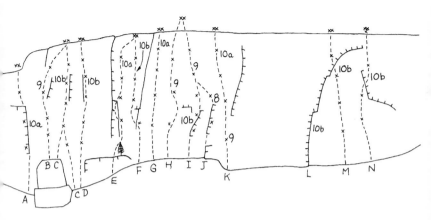

UPPER RIGHT WING

A	Knight Shift	10a	
B	Cameo*	9	
C	Diamond Sky*	10b	
D	Charm*	10b	
E	Blind Faith	10a	
F	Silhouette*	10b	
G	Tapdance*	10a/b	
H	Yellow Wedge*	9	
I	Lemon Pie*	10b	
J	Lime Street*	9	
K	Pink Cadillac**	10a	
L	Pitrun*	10b	gear to 2.5"
M	Caught in the Crossfire**	10b	
N	Supplication*	10b	

The Alley is reached by turning right at the base of The Headwall and scrambling up a steep trail on the right side of the creek. Head up and away from the creek at the first obvious opportunity. **BE EXTREMELY CAREFUL NOT TO DISLODGE ROCKS FROM THE TRAIL AS THEY COULD INJURE HIKERS BELOW**.

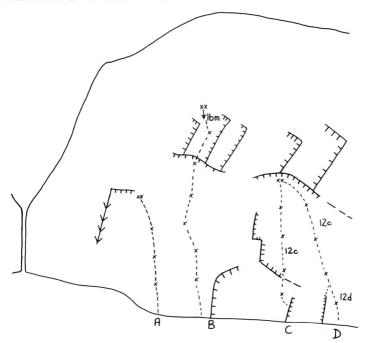

THE ALLEY, LEFT

A	Hee Haw	12b/c
B	Scream Saver	12a
C	White Noise**	12c
D	A Fetching Bell Shape, Small But Perfectly Formed**	12c or d

Barb Clemes on Success Pool (12a),
Grotto Canyon (p. 188). Photo Brian Bailey.

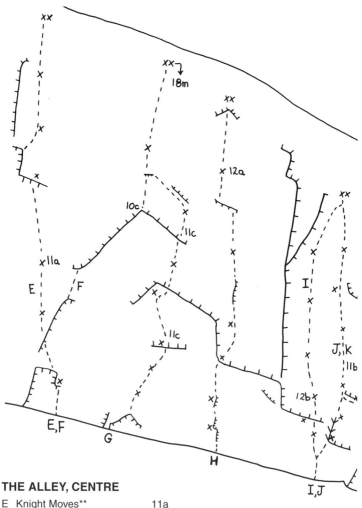

THE ALLEY, CENTRE

E	Knight Moves**	11a
F	Hollow Victory	10c
G	Barchetta**	11c
H	Path of the Moose	12a
I	Get Your Ducks in a Row**	12b
J	Submission Direct**	11b

gear to 2.5"

THE ALLEY, RIGHT

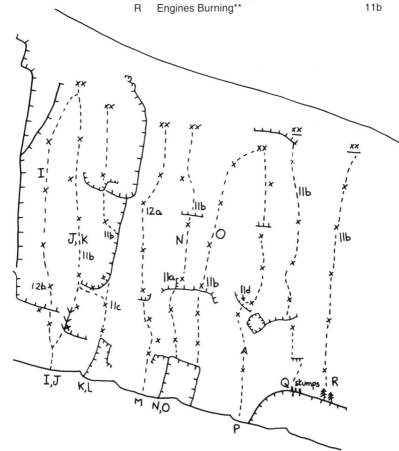

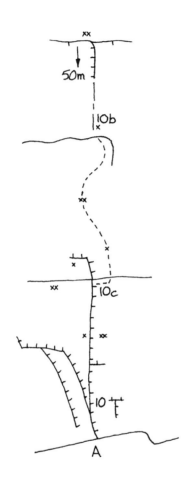

THE HEADWALL

A   The Verdict*   10c   gear to 3"

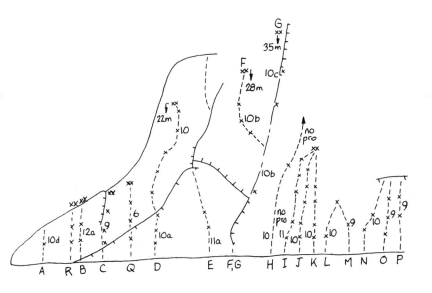

LOWER NARROWS

A	Bogus	10d	
B	Mighty Mite*	12a	
C	The Midden	9	gear to 2"
D	Xanadu**	10a/b	
E	Stormy Weather	11a	gear to Friend 3
F	Blik	10b	gear to Friend 3
G	West Coast Idea*	10c	gear to Friend 3
H	Moonabago	10b	not recommended
I	Mendocino*	11a	
J	Malibu*	10c	
K	Monterey*	10a	
L	Baker Street	10d	
M	Dr Watson	9	
N	Lost World	10a	
O	Hollow Earth	9	
P	Moriarty	9	
Q	unknown	6	
R	Mighty Mark	12b	

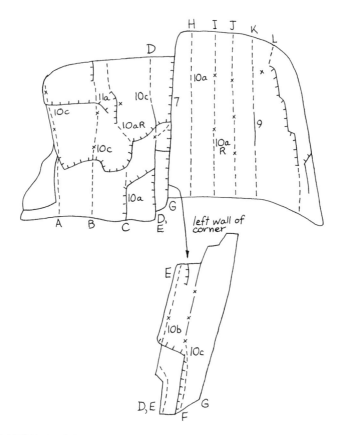

ILLUSION ROCK

A	Harder Than It Looks	10c	
B	Monkey in a Rage*	11a	
C	Grand Illusion*	10a	
D	Grander Illusion*	10c	RPs, small wired nuts
E	Guitarzan*	10b	
F	George of the Jungle*	10c	
G	Jackorner*	7	gear to 3"
H	Zapped	10a	use G to protect
I	Impending Impact*	10a	
J	Smooth Move	10a/b	
K	Tiny Tim	9	
L	Yonge Street	8	

Delusion Rock is a couple of minutes uphill from the top of Illusion Rock.

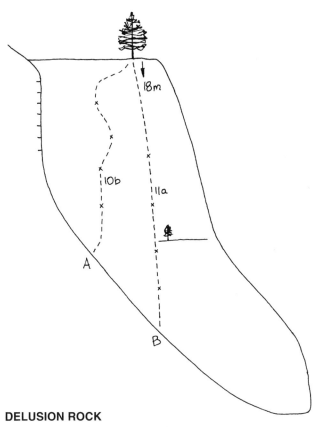

DELUSION ROCK

A Burnt Weenie Sandwich*   10b
B Grand Delusion*   11a

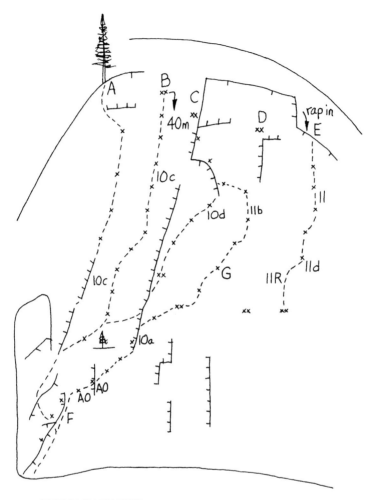

UPPER NARROWS

A	Trading Places*	10c	small wires, Friends, TCUs
B	Undertow*	10c	small wires, Friend 2
C	Tabernaquered*	10d	small wires, Friend 2
D	open project		
E	Mirage	11d	rap to start
F	Neorevisionist*	10a A0	
G	Magical Mystery Tour**	11b	

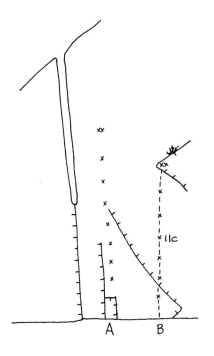

EXIT WALL

A open project
B Blackened   11c

The **Upper Tier** is a textured slab high up on the east side of the canyon just beyond the end of The Narrows. Walk about 150 m past the upstream end of The Narrows and start up at a little scree slope on the right side near a small, yellowish outcrop of glacial till. Work up and right past short, slabby cliff bands, then up and left through woods to reach the climbs—about 15 minutes from the valley floor.

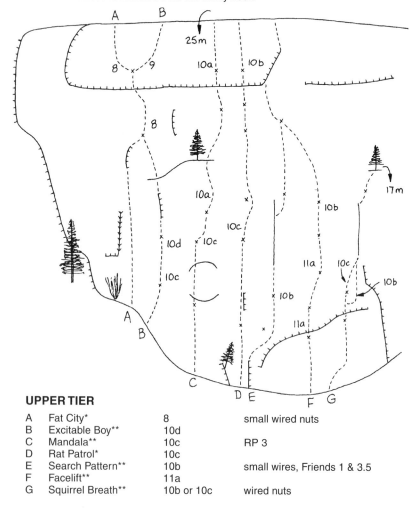

UPPER TIER

A	Fat City*	8	small wired nuts
B	Excitable Boy**	10d	
C	Mandala**	10c	RP 3
D	Rat Patrol*	10c	
E	Search Pattern**	10b	small wires, Friends 1 & 3.5
F	Facelift**	11a	
G	Squirrel Breath**	10b or 10c	wired nuts

Garden Rock is a small cliff in the valley bottom just beyond a large cave in the glacial till formations on the west side of the valley.

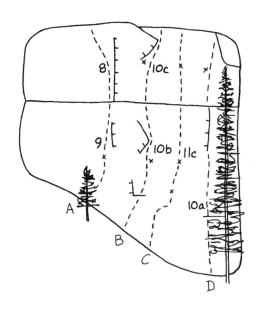

GARDEN ROCK

A	Pining Away*	9	wired nuts
B	Conifer Crack**	10c	Friend 3
C	Chainsaw Wall	11c	
D	All Spruced Up*	10a	small wired nuts, RPs

Hoodoo Crag is just beyond Garden Rock on the same side of the valley and about 75 m up from the valley floor. The easiest approach starts at the base of Armadillo Buttress, the large cliff just beyond Garden Rock. Work up and left, following the base of Armadillo Buttress at first, for about 5 minutes to get to the cliff.

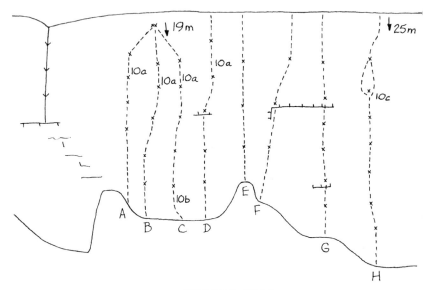

HOODOO CRAG

A	Hoodlum*	10a
B	Hoodunit*	10a
C	Hoodini*	10b
D	Hoodoo You Love?*	10a
E	Deadly Buds	10b
F	Hoor Tour	10d
G	Who're You?	11b
H	Hoodoo Voodoo**	10c

Grotto Slab, a low-angle friction climbing area, is reached by following scraps of trail in the creek valley about 15 minutes upstream from Hoodoo Crag. The climbs are at the far end of the slab. Bring two ropes!

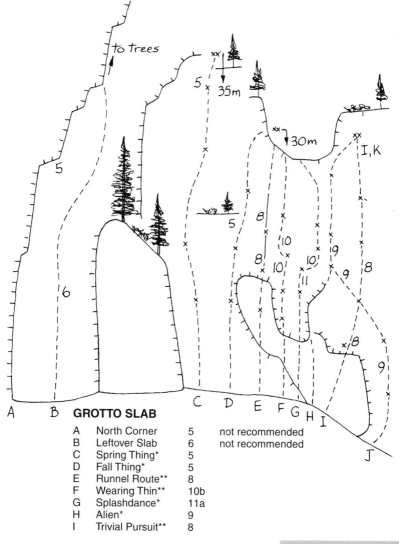

GROTTO SLAB

A	North Corner	5	not recommended
B	Leftover Slab	6	not recommended
C	Spring Thing*	5	
D	Fall Thing*	5	
E	Runnel Route**	8	
F	Wearing Thin**	10b	
G	Splashdance*	11a	
H	Alien*	9	
I	Trivial Pursuit**	8	

GROTTO SLAB

J	The Stand**	9
K	Central Park*	6
L	Space Cadet*	6
M	Spacewalk*	7
N	Cody for Mayor*	7
O	Afternoon Delight*	5
P	Old School Wannabe*	6
Q	Cruisin' for Burgers*	4
R	Patty's Climb*	4 gear to Friend 3

Aqua Slab is immediately right of Grotto Slab.

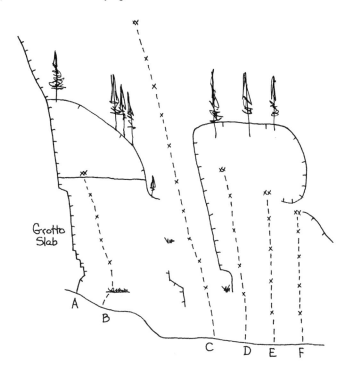

AQUA SLAB

A	Patty's Climb	4	gear
B	Latacunga	7	
C	Riobamba*	10a	
D	Snore Kling	7	
E	Swallow Your Pride	7	
F	Sea Horesing	7	

Silk Cuts is at the far right end of the Grotto Slab outcrop.

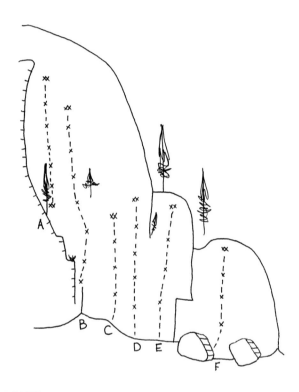

SILK CUTS

A	Bolivian*	7
B	Pushin' a Space Broom**	7
C	Gotta Eagle to Feed	7
D	Fallen Palms*	5
E	Frankenclimbz	7
F	Captains Courageous*	8

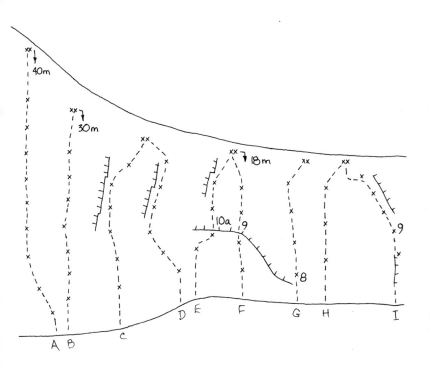

THE UNCHARTED SEA

A 30 Minute Famine**   7
B Like a Big-wall Climber from Modesto
    Who's Never Been to Yosemite**   5
C Teflon Ocean Wall   8
D Barbecued Planet   7
E Poop-a-si-a   10a
F Leave Something Witchie   9
G Kamloops for Breakfast   8
H Iron Knickers   9
I Crypt Trip   9+

Steve Canyon is the next watercourse east of Grotto Canyon. This scenic and easily accessible little area is seldom visited by climbers, but it does have a few worthwhile routes. The cliffs face east and get morning sun.

Approach

Park north of Highway 1A at Grotto Mountain day-use area, 3.4 km west of the service station in Exshaw. Look for an unsigned trail in trees on the west side of the parking lot. Follow this 2 - 3 minutes to a watercourse. The watercourse can also be reached from the powerline road (signed as the Grotto Canyon Trail). Follow the watercourse uphill for 10 – 15 minutes past a picturesquely sculptured waterslide to reach the Bathtub Crags, which sport a waterfall at the far end. The Upper Wall lies above the waterfall and can be reached from the top of the Bathtub Crags or by an awkward scramble to the right of the waterfall.

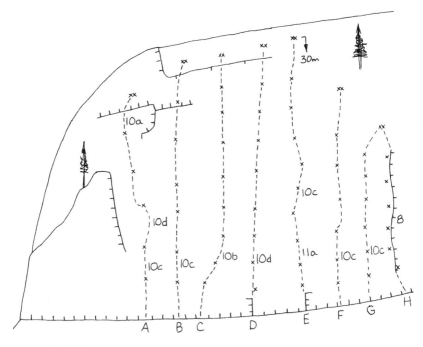

UPPER WALL

A	Devil May Care**	10d	E	Timeless**	11a
B	Dream Weaver**	10c	F	Unfinished Sympathy*	10c
C	Take Five**	10b	G	Crystal Silence*	10c
D	All That Jazz*	10d	H	Friendly Persuasion*	8

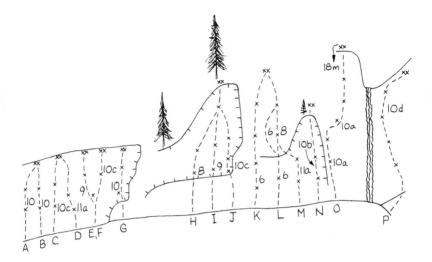

LOWER CRAGS

A	Nervous Tick	10b
B	Pumpkin Smasher	10b
C	Where's the Beef?	10c
D	Bermuda Triangle	11a
E	Tickicide	9
F	Tickicide Direct	10c
G	Dr Tongue's 3D House of Beef	10a
H	Bozoids from Planet X	8
I	The Bozone Layer	9
J	X-Files	10c
K	Deadhead Left	6
L	Deadhead Right	6 or 8
M	The Lump	11a
N	The Hump*	10b
O	The Devil Drives*	10a
P	Moist and Easy*	10d

THE SANCTUARY

This is a long, south-facing, two-tiered cliff above and east of Steve Canyon. The cliffs are deceptively steep, and although the routes are mostly short, they tend to be fierce. The Sanctuary is in the sun nearly all day and thus is a good early spring and late fall destination. Take water; there is none on the approach or at the cliff.

Approach

Turn north on the Baymag #2 road, 3.7 km west of the service station in Exshaw. After 100 m park at the powerline road. From here The Sanctuary is visible as a pale cliff, slanting from lower left to upper right, on the right side of a drainage (Steve Canyon) directly in front of you. Start as for the alternate Steve Canyon approach by walking east on the powerline road about 1 minute, then taking a trail that branches left. In about 1 more minute the trail crosses the drainage from Steve Canyon and starts up a steep hill. Continue up the trail, first through woods and then up a ridge, for about 40 minutes. Just beyond a steep, rocky section the trail comes out on scree slopes on the left side of the ridge. Watch for a faint trail heading left across the slope. This trail leads to The Sanctuary in 7 - 8 minutes more, reaching Left Cliff near *Instinct*. Lower Cliff is up the trail about 50 m. The approach trail up the ridge can just as easily be reached from the Grotto Mountain day-use area (see Steve Canyon approach), but The Sanctuary is not visible for orientation.

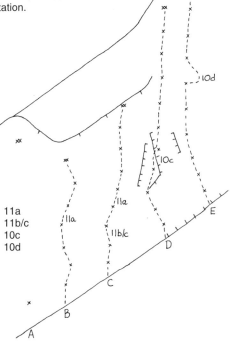

LEFT CLIFF

A	project	
B	Instinct*	11a
C	Just a Motion Away*	11b/c
D	Autumn Leaves*	10c
E	String of Pearls**	10d

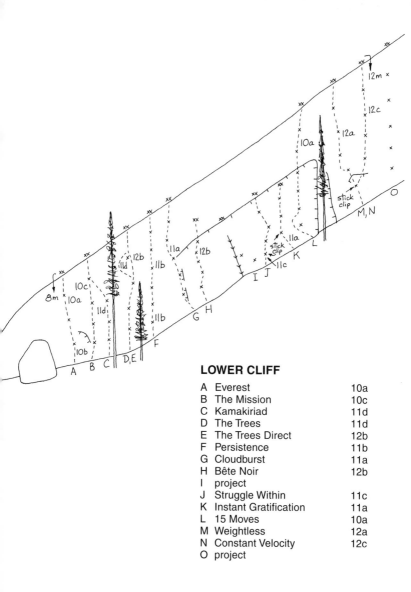

LOWER CLIFF

A	Everest	10a
B	The Mission	10c
C	Kamakiriad	11d
D	The Trees	11d
E	The Trees Direct	12b
F	Persistence	11b
G	Cloudburst	11a
H	Bête Noir	12b
I	project	
J	Struggle Within	11c
K	Instant Gratification	11a
L	15 Moves	10a
M	Weightless	12a
N	Constant Velocity	12c
O	project	

O

P

G.

KID GOAT

KID GOAT AND NANNY GOAT

Kid Goat is the southernmost and smallest of the east-facing cliffs on the south ridge of Goat Mountain, the prominent peak that forms the mountain front immediately southwest of Yamnuska. Nanny Goat is the next cliff north. Both cliffs offer an unusual style of climbing on rough-textured rock. Because of their orientation, the cliffs warm up early in the morning but go out of the sun in early afternoon. It is also worth noting that they seep badly for a couple of days after rain. The routes on Kid Goat are fully equipped but gear is needed for Nanny Goat. Take two ropes for either destination.

Approach

Park at a paved pull-off on the south side of Highway 1A a short distance east of the mountain front. Cross the highway and follow a gravel road to an intersection. The right fork leads to the regional landfill site and is gated. If the gate is open, follow the road until it turns left, then cross a fence directly ahead and angle left to pick up a gravel track. If the gate is closed, cross the fence on the right (east) of the road, and follow a trail that parallels the road to the point where it turns left. Gain the gravel track as in the other option. Follow this track a short distance through trees, turn left on another gravel track and continue to a small gravel extraction site. Above, the track steepens significantly. This steep section is clearly visible in the centre bottom of the photo. To get to Kid Goat, continue up the track, which soon narrows to trail width. At a fork in the trail you can continue straight up or branch left. To get to Nanny Goat, look for a faint trail that contours along the slope to the right soon after the track steepens. Follow this trail through a short section of forest to the watercourse that descends from the gully between Kid Goat and Nanny Goat (the watercourse is easily found even if you miss this section of trail). The trail now turns straight uphill, following first the left side of the watercourse and then the right. When you reach Nanny Goat, the *Predator* Area will be immediately to your right. The approach to either Kid Goat or Nanny Goat takes about 40 minutes. Nanny Goat is easily accessible in about 5 minutes from Kid Goat and vice-versa.

Opposite: G Gray Waves,   P Predator Area,   O Overnight Sensation.

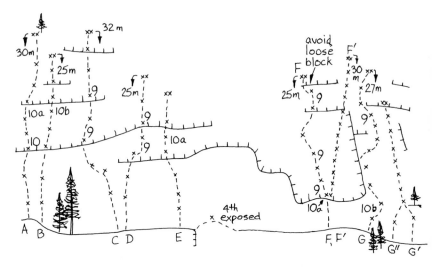

KID GOAT

A	True Stories*	10a/b
B	Lies and Whispers*	10b
C	Coarse and Juggy**	9
D	Dawntreader*	9
E	The Swell*	10a
F	Half Life*	9
F'	The Beat Goes On*	10a
G	Smoking Mirror**	10b
G'	As If	10a
G"	alt. start	11a

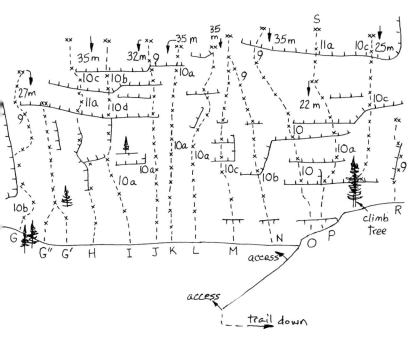

KID GOAT

G	Smoking Mirror**	10b
H	Wave Goodbye**	11a
I	Max Headroom**	10d
J	Diehard*	10a
K	New Hope for the Dead**	10a
L	Talk Dirty to Me**	10a
M	Takedown**	10c
N	Feeding Frenzy**	10b
O	Divers from the Anaerobic Zone*	10b
P	Shakedown*	10a
Q	Syzygy**	10c
R	Slow Hand	9
S	Breakdown*	11a

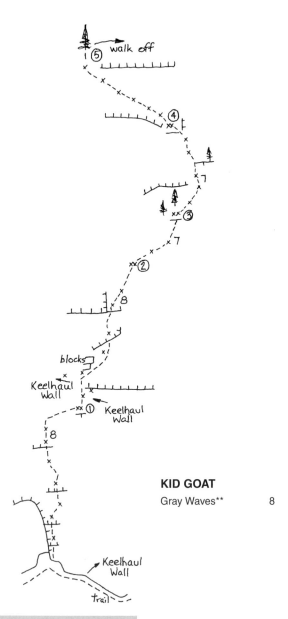

walk off

blocks

Keelhaul
Wall

Keelhaul
Wall

8

KID GOAT

Gray Waves**   8

Keelhaul
Wall

trail

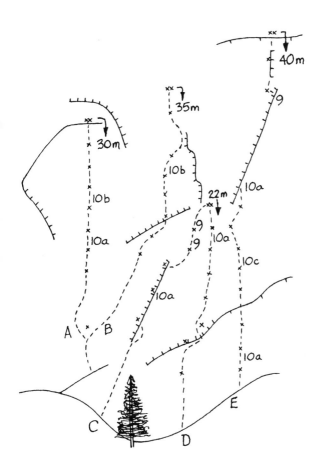

NANNY GOAT, PREDATOR AREA

A	Peep Show**	10b	
B	Blue Movie*	10b	Rocks 1-2
C	Fadeout*	10a	Rock 3
D	Freeze Frame*	10a	
E	Predator**	10c	Rocks 1-8, Friends 1-4

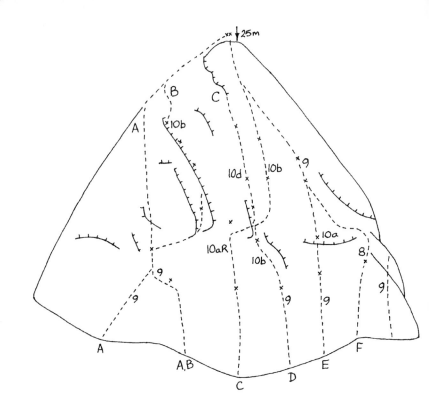

NANNY GOAT, OVERNIGHT SENSATION AREA

A	Nightland*	9	small Rocks
B	Bedtime Story*	10b	
C	Overnight Sensation	10d	
D	Into the Night*	10b	
D/C	Night Sensation**	10d	
E	Evening Star*	10a	
F	Nightcap	9	Friend 1.5

YAMNUSKA

Six of the many routes on Yamnuska are included in this guide. With the exception of *Bringers of the Dawn* they are not sport climbs. However, these routes have more fixed protection and better belays than most on Yamnuska and may be of interest to those sport climbers who are confident enough to place a bit of protection and run it out a little bit more than on most of the other climbs in this guide. There is rockfall hazard on Yamnuska—**WEAR A HELMET.**

Approach

There is a new approach to Yamnuska. Turn off as before on the quarry access road, which leaves Highway 1A about 2 km east of the junction with Highway 1X. Keep left at a Y junction and shortly afterward turn left into the new parking area. Take the new trail, which leaves from the west end of the parking lot, cross the access road (now gated) in less than 100 m and continue to a fork near the right end of the quarry. Stay left. The trail angles up and left, above the quarry, and eventually intersects the switchbacks of the original trail. From the parking lot it takes about 45 - 60 minutes to get to the cliffs. From the top of the trail, *Gormenghast* and *CMC Wall* are to the west (left); *Bringers of the Dawn*, *Dreambed* and *Snert's Big Adventure* are to the east (right).

Gormenghast starts just west of the prominent line of *Grillmair Chimney*. Follow the trail west along the base of the cliff for a few minutes across the top of a large scree bowl. Immediately beyond this, scramble up and right through short walls and scree ledges to the base of a short, steep wall. Start in a shallow, clean, right-facing corner with three stainless steel bolt hangers on its right. The prominent chimney system visible at the top of the crag directly above is *Chockstone Corner*.

To reach *CMC Wall*, continue west on the trail past *Gormenghast* to a point below the prominent left-slanting break of *Calgary Route*. Scramble up and right until just past the start of that route. Continue up an easy chimney to the top of a small buttress. A careful search may turn up an old bolt, which marks the start. Double ropes lessen rope drag and make retreat possible. The alternative 4th pitch is superior, but is much harder and is more runout than the original 4th and 5th pitches. The alternative 6th pitch, but the original 7th and 8th pitches, are recommended. *Super SOAG* starts just right of *CMC Wall*.

Bringers of the Dawn starts 30 m right of where the trail reaches the cliff. *Dreambed* starts about 4 minutes farther east and *Snert's Big Adventure* is about 3 - 4 minutes farther east again.

CW

SB

DB

GC BD

GG

GG

BD
Approach
Trail

SB

DB

BD

GG

CR CW

CR Calgary Route   CW CMC Wall   BD Bringers of the Dawn   SB Snert's Big Adventure
GC Grillmair Chimney GG Gormenghast   DB Dreambed

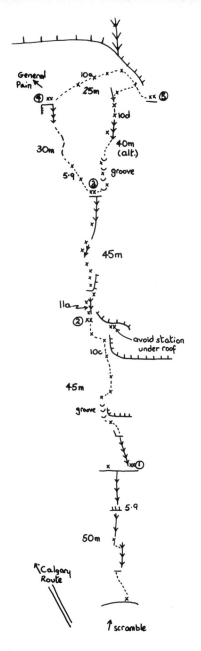

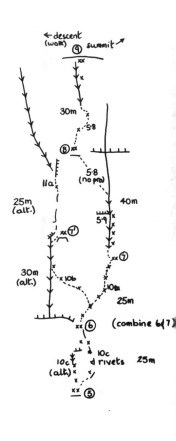

CMC Wall** 11a
gear to 3", RPs, TCUs

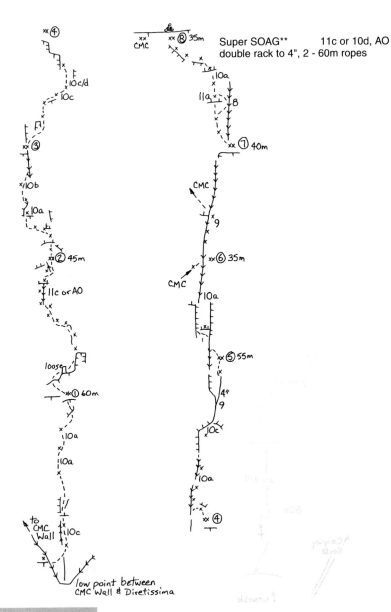

Super SOAG** 11c or 10d, AO
double rack to 4", 2 - 60m ropes

xx ④

10c/d
10c

xx ③

x/10b

x 10a

xx ② 45m

11c or AO

loose

x ① 60m

10a

10a

to
CMC
Wall 10c

low point between
CMC Wall & Diretissima

xx ⑧ 35m
CMC

10a

11a 8

xx ⑦ 40m

CMC

9

xx ⑥ 35m

CMC

10a

xx ⑤ 55m

4"
9

10c

10a

xx ④

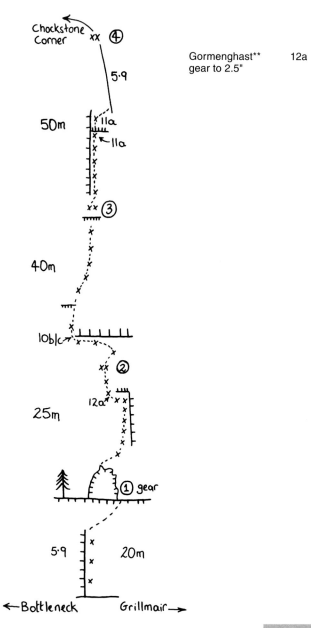

Gormenghast**   12a
gear to 2.5"

Chockstone
Corner

④

5·9

50m   11a
      11a

xx ③

40m

10b/c

xx ②

12a

25m

① gear

5·9   20m

←Bottleneck   Grillmair→

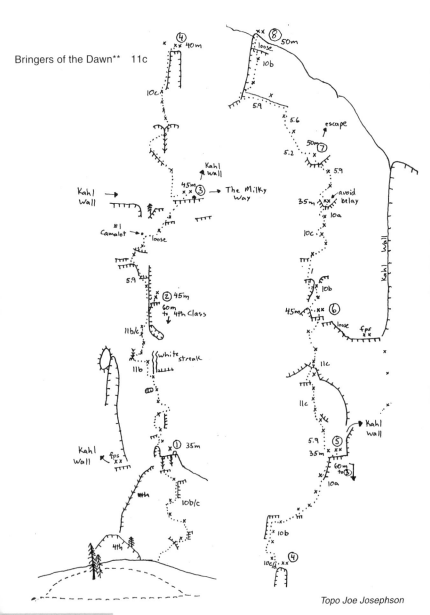

Bringers of the Dawn** 11c

Topo Joe Josephson

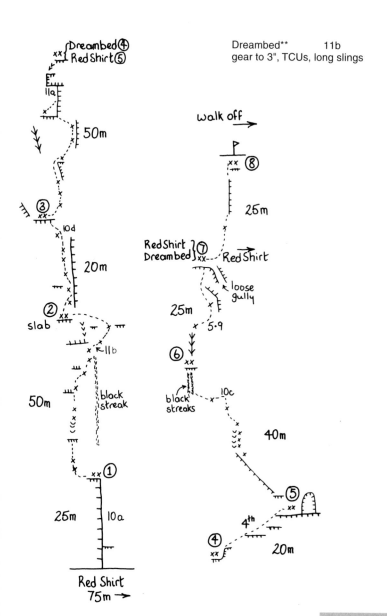

Dreambed ④
Red Shirt ⑤

Dreambed**   11b
gear to 3", TCUs, long slings

walk off →

⑧
25m

Red Shirt ⑦
Dreambed → Red Shirt
loose gully
25m
5·9

11a

50m

③

10d

20m

②
slab

11b

50m

black streak

①

25m   10a

⑥
black streaks   10c

40m

⑤
4th
④   20m

Red Shirt
75m →

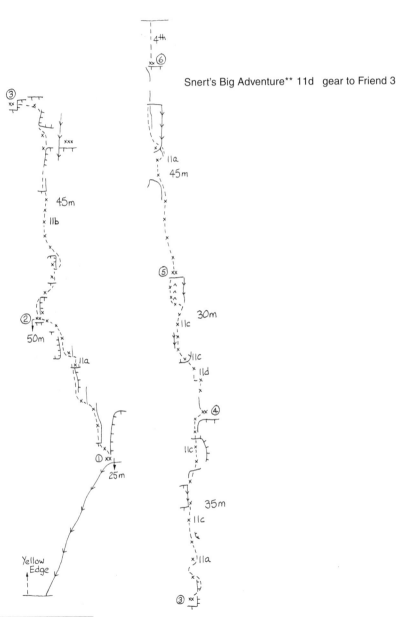

Snert's Big Adventure** 11d   gear to Friend 3

③
xx

45m
IIb

45m

4th
⑥ xx

IIa
45m

⑤ xx
30m
IIc

IIc
IId

xx ④

② xx
50m
IIa

IIc
35m
IIc

① xx
25m

IIa

③ xx

Yellow
Edge

Peter Arbic on pitch 1,
Dreams of Verdon, (11+),
Ghost (p. 242). Photo Roger
Chayer/Talus Photographics.

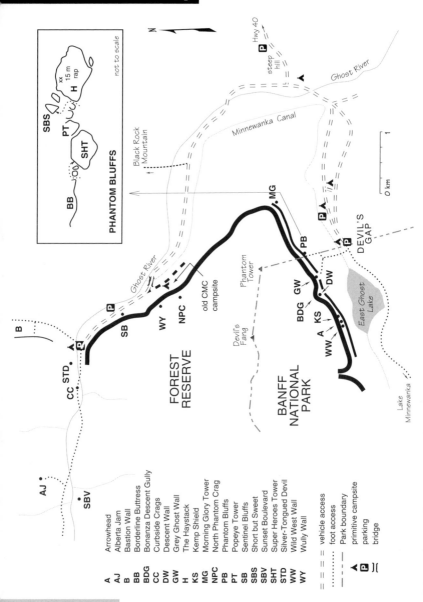

PHANTOM BLUFFS

not to scale

SBS
PT
H   15 m
       rap
xx
SHT
BB

Black Rock Mountain

N

Hwy 40
steep hill

Ghost River

Minnewanka Canal

O km   1

MG

PB

DEVIL'S GAP

Ghost River

P

DW
GW
BDG
KS
A
WW

East Ghost Lake

Phantom Tower

SB
WY
NPC

old CMC campsite

FOREST RESERVE

BANFF NATIONAL PARK

Devil's Fang

Lake Minnewanka

B

CC STD.

AJ

SBV

A   Arrowhead
AJ   Alberta Jam
B   Bastion Wall
BB   Borderline Buttress
BDG Bonanza Descent Gully
CC   Curbside Crags
DW   Descent Wall
GW   Grey Ghost Wall
H   The Haystack
KS   Kemp Shield
MG   Morning Glory Tower
NPC North Phantom Crag
PB   Phantom Bluffs
PT   Popeye Tower
SB   Sentinel Bluffs
SBS Short but Sweet
SBV Sunset Boulevard
SHT Super Heroes Tower
STD Silver-Tongued Devil
WW   Wild West Wall
WY   Wully Wall

= = = = vehicle access
. . . . foot access
— · —   Park boundary
. . . . primitive campsite
P   parking
] [bridge

The amount of high quality rock and potential for new routes in this area is staggering. There are routes of all kinds here, from sport climbs to traditional climbs, and from 15 m to 300 m in length. The Ghost is home to *Dreams of Verdon*, which is arguably the best multi-pitch sport route in the area. Some of the climbs described below, particularly the older ones, require placement of some protection and may be more runout than the average canyon sport climb. Also, some of the older climbs, particularly those on Kemp Shield and Sentinel Bluffs, are equipped with home-made hangers that require low profile biners to clip. The areas included below are those where there are the highest concentrations of sport/semi-sport routes. The climbs are mostly single-pitch, but some require 2 ropes to descend. Several new multi-pitch sport climbs are described and two recent well-protected, multi-pitch gear routes, that the confident sport climber might enjoy, are also included. Complete coverage of the rock climbs in this area may be found in *Ghost Rock* (1997) by Joe Josephson, Chris Perry and Andy Genereux.

Most of the crags have scree ledges above the climbs, and so the use of helmets is advised. Some crags are isolated and rarely visited, so you should tell someone where you are going before climbing here as there may not be anyone around to respond to calls for help in the case of an emergency (**RCMP** Cochrane 403-932-2211). Cell phone coverage is patchy in the Ghost and the nearest phone over an hour away from the climbs. This is a relatively *remote* climbing area and a rescue may be slow in arriving and difficult to effect, so be prepared.

Camping

One of the best features of the Ghost is the abundance of good, free camping, making this an ideal destination for the weekend. You can camp anywhere in the Ghost outside of Banff National Park, which prohibits any camping or overnighting. There are, however, several established campsites where most people reside. They are located as follows: 1) at the bottom of the Big Hill on the left, 2) along the park boundary in Devil's Gap, 3) next to the river near the Black Rock hiking trail, 4) at the old Calgary Mountain Club (CMC) campsite near Wully Wall, and 5) in the clearing near the start of the Bastion Wall approach. These areas are marked on the map on page 206. All of these areas have numerous little niches and clearings that make for fine camping.

Water

Except for the Big Hill campsite, all sites have access to water most of the summer. During spring runoff or flood, there will be water near the Big Hill. Before spring thaw and late in the season the river in Devil's Gap will dry up. To the authors' knowledge, all water in the Ghost is fit to drink as is. If you are unsure or concerned, boil or filter it.

Fire

Most well-established campsites will have fire rings, many of them outlandishly big. If you have a fire, please use an established ring. **Do not** make new fire rings or build fires directly on the ground. The ground cover in the area is very fragile. Some areas, particularly Devil's Gap, are starting to get picked clean of dead wood. **Do not cut down any trees for firewood, either living or dead-standing**. Find deadfall or better yet bring your own. During extreme fire hazards, the forest service may restrict camp fires on

Andy Genereux on Boy Wonder (11c),
Ghost River Area (p. 252). Photo Jon Jones.

Crown lands. As there are no services in the Ghost, you are responsible for knowing when fires are not allowed. Call the Ghost Ranger Station at 403-297-8800.

Human Waste

There are no outhouses in the Ghost River area. When nature calls, walk at least 200 m from any streams, climbing or camping sites and find an out of the way place, preferably in the trees. It is best to bury your waste in 6 - 8 inches of topsoil and burn the toilet paper. Better yet, desecrate a trash bag and carry all the waste out with you. At the very least you should burn the paper. The most popular campsites in Devil's Gap are beginning to see white flowers (toilet paper and tampons) scattered through the trees. In general, however, waste has not been a big problem. **Please—it is up to us to keep it that way.**

Garbage

Put only combustible material into a camp fire. This **does not** include plastic, tin foil, tin cans or batteries. If you do burn tins to rid them of food odours, pack them out with the rest of your garbage. By keeping our impact minimal and our profile low, we can do our part to help maintain the unrestricted access we now enjoy, but more importantly we can endeavour to preserve the fragile ground cover and ecosystem of the Ghost. Besides, none of us really want to find a pigsty when we go camping.

Access

The main areas are 75 - 90 minutes drive from either Calgary or Canmore, followed by a 20 - 40 minute walk. From Calgary, follow Highway 1A (Crowchild Trail) west to the junction with Secondary Road 940 (aka the Forestry Trunk Road or Highway 40) 14 km west of Cochrane.

From Canmore/Banff, the quickest route is to follow Highway 1 east to the Chief Chiniki/Morley turn-off and then Morley Road north to Highway 1A. Here turn right and go 15.5 km east (4 km past Ghost Dam) to the junction with SR 940.

Follow SR 940 for about 25 km (passing the hamlet of Waiparous), to a sharp bend at the junction with Richards Road. Continue 100 m and then turn left onto a gravel road with a cattle grid and gate. **Please re-close the gate if you found it closed!** Bear right at a fork after 3 km, just beyond a small bridge and cattle grid. Continue west for another 13.5 km to a viewpoint at the top of the "Big Hill." Ahead and slightly left (west) is Devil's Gap and the Minnewanka Valley; ahead and to the right (northwest) is the Ghost River valley. The southern group of crags included in this guide (Phantom Bluffs, Grey Ghost Wall, Descent Wall, The Kemp Shield, The Arrowhead and Wild West Wall) are on the north side of the Minnewanka Valley. The northern group of crags (North Phantom Crag, Wully Wall, Sentinel Bluffs, Silver-Tongued Devil Crag, Bastion Wall, Alberta Jam and Sunset Boulevard) are located in the Ghost River valley.

Most vehicles should make it this far without any problems, but the road down the Big Hill is now very rough. If your vehicle is not up to it, park on the right at the top of the hill and walk or bike the rest of the way. The walking time from here to the parking area for the southern group of crags is about 30 minutes while it will take you over an hour to reach the parking area for Silver-Tongued Devil Crag on foot.

At the bottom of the hill is a sign, "Black Rock Lookout Hiking Trail." **Driving distances (in brackets) that follow are *from this point*.**

WARNING: The Ghost River is subject to sudden flooding, especially in spring but also after heavy summer rain showers. To quote *Ghost Rock*, "The river bed along the base of the Big Hill is usually dry but can at times be a raging torrent. If this is the case, don't even attempt to cross by car or foot. More importantly, these floods change (i.e. eliminate) roads, carve steep banks and give the Ghost its sometimes deserved reputation for difficult access. It is recommended that you have good clearance or a 4WD. Faint tracks and roads abound in the Ghost. If a section ahead looks impassable, you can usually find an alternative. Take your time and if in doubt, scout ahead or walk. All parking areas are a 15 - 30 minute drive from the Big Hill if you don't get stuck."

Approach to the Minnewanka Valley—Devil's Gap Crags

From the bottom of the hill, bear left and follow a track a short distance along the east side of the river bed to a steep break in the bank that leads to the river bed. Follow a track angling south (downstream) until it is possible to gain the west bank near the left end of a long section of wire-covered riprap (boulders). Climb out of the river bed via another steep bank and follow a good road south for about 100 m to where it swings west. Shortly after this is a 3-way junction at a peeling green sign (which comes and goes over the years!). Take the middle road. This bends left, goes down the bank, crosses the flats and then winds through trees (some deeply rutted and muddy sections) to a large sign indicating the boundary of Banff National Park. **Vehicles are prohibited beyond this point**. Make a sharp right turn and follow a good track a short distance to a parking area in a meadow by the river.

Phantom Bluffs comprise the right end of the narrow band of light grey rock, just below the spectacular main rock face opposite. The remaining crags included in this section are on the main cliffs above (West Phantom Crags in *Ghost Rock* p. 59) 1 - 2 km farther west.

To approach the Phantom Bluffs and West Phantom Crags, walk about 100 m downstream (west) from the Banff Park boundary (identified by yellow pickets) until opposite a break in the far riverbank that is just downstream from a prominent earth scar. Wade the river and follow a game trail on the other side that leads up a shallow, dry, treed ravine to where the ravine floor flattens and curves round to the right (east). Here climb the steep slope on the left via 3 or 4 switchbacks to an open shoulder. From here the trail heads leftwards. Follow it a short distance into the trees to a cairn where a trail branches off to the right. To get to Phantom Bluffs, take this trail to the right. For West Phantom Crags, continue on the trail that heads left from the cairn.

The trail to Phantom Bluffs contours right from the cairn for about 200 m to the Banff National Park boundary cut line (prominent cairn). Phantom Bluffs are at the head of this cut line. You will probably arrive at the right end of Borderline Buttress (about 20 - 25 minutes from the parking area).

Morning Glory Tower is reached from The Haystack (Phantom Bluffs area—see map). Traverse right through open trees (no trail) and drop down slightly below a small shattered crag consisting of two towers. Continue traversing across a treed slope to a shallow bowl in the hillside and then to open slopes beyond. The back (west) side of Morning Glory Tower should now be visible to the east. The climbs are on the east side.

KS	Kemp Shield	GW	Grey Ghost Wall		*Minnewanka Valley.*
WW	Wild West Wall	PB	Phantom Bluffs	MG	Morning Glory Tower
BDG	Bonanza Descent Gully	△	cairn at fork in trail		(not visible)

To get to the West Phantom Crags from the cairn at the split in the trail, continue on the prominent trail that diagonals left (west) across the slope and then switchbacks up through an obvious break in the rock band above. (*Southern Exposure* starts 50 m uphill, directly above this point.)

Ghost River Valley Crags Approach

Turn right at the bottom of the steep hill and follow a good road that parallels the riverbank. The traditional river crossing was at a cable crossing about 1 km from the bottom of the Big Hill, but floods have eroded a very steep embankment that, at the time of writing (2002), is impassable to all vehicles except 4WDs with high clearance. Drivers of other vehicles will have to seek an alternative crossing somewhere before this point. Scout your crossing *carefully* beforehand though—a submerged 4WD is not an uncommon sight here during floods! Once on the other (west) side, continue northwestwards on a good gravel road, passing the Black Rock Mountain Hiking Trail sign (2.3 km) to the bridge over the diversion canal (4.3 km).

Wully Wall

This is best reached from the general vicinity of the old CMC campsite (see map p. 234). Just after crossing the bridge across the canal, turn sharply to the left onto a road that parallels the canal. Wully Wall, the face now directly above you on the right, is best accessed using the approach to *Consolation* described in *Ghost Rock* (p. 172):

"To reach the *Consolation* area, turn left toward the CMC campsite and locate a small side road on the right, about 250 m south of the canal bridge, that leads to a small clearing in the trees (campsite). Starting from here, the easiest approach is via a small, overgrown gully that leads up to a scree cone immediately to the right of the route. The gully is difficult to find from below and is best located just before you pull into the side road. The gully lies about 75 m north of the parking for the campsite. A faint trail climbs its right bank and then moves over left near the top."

The multi-pitch sport climb *Trace* (p. 258) is the rightmost climb on Wully Wall.

North Phantom Crag

North Phantom Crag lies to the southeast (left) of Wully Wall and is separated from it by the deep drainage of Wully Canyon. Several excellent sport climbs have been established on its Right End in the general vicinity of the mega-classic *Dirty Dancing* (see *Ghost Rock*, p. 162-5). To reach these climbs, continue on the road that parallels the canal until it becomes impassable (near the old CMC campsite, about 400 m from the bridge). Park here and follow a washed-out road that heads up the hill into an old gravel pit. Cross the pit and then follow the small stream that drains Wully Canyon upstream through a small gorge to where the canyon opens up and the drainage begins to curve round to the north (right) (about 10 minutes from parking). Here climb easily up the steep slope on the left to the base of the main cliff. Follow a good trail left that more or less contours across the slope from here for about 10 - 15 minutes, crossing a couple of rocky ribs on the way, to an open scree slope where the trail becomes less distinct. Continue traversing left, well below a large, rectangular buttress (this is *Square Buttress*, see p. 259) at the base of the cliff to a scree slope that leads up and right and back to the main cliff below the unmistakable clean cut right-facing corner systems of the middle section of *Dirty Dancing* (about 30 minutes from parking). (A more detailed description of this approach appears in *Ghost Rock*, p. 159.) The excellent sport climbs *Smokin' in the Boys Room* (p. 260) and *Don't Forget to Dance* (p. 261) are located 30 and 40 m right of *Dirty Dancing* respectively and are separated by a "tunnel" through the ridge that joins the main crag to the back of *Square Buttress*.

Sentinel Bluffs: From the bridge across the diversion canal, continue northwest on the main road through the trees until it opens up and a small road merges from behind on the right (about 0.9 km from the bridge). 50 m past this road, a steep scree gully leads up through the trees to Sentinel Bluffs (only the uppermost part of which is visible from the road). Park about 150 m beyond here in a clearing on the right (5.4 km) opposite a large scree cone that has a prominent debris flow track on its right side. Head up the hillside just left of this scree gully on an indistinct and discontinuous trail. Cut diagonally leftwards across the wooded slope and then climb steeply up the crest of the broad ridge between the two scree gullies until it is possible to cut left to the base of Sentinel Bluffs, arriving near the route *The Surprise*. The 20 - 30 minute hike up to the crag has been succinctly described by Andy Skuce as, "Bush-Moss-Scree-Pain."

(**Note:** Many of the climbs on Sentinel Bluffs are *not* sport climbs. Even those that are fully bolted date from the early days of sport climbs and some are *very* run-out by modern standards! Also, wait for warm, dry weather before climbing here as the cliff is in the shade from mid-morning onwards.)

Silver-Tongued Devil Crag: About 6 km from the bottom of the Big Hill, the main Ghost River access road "ends" at the rocky flats where the Ghost River makes a 90-degree turn to the west. Silver-Tongued Devil Crag is the impressive cliff opposite, directly above the river bend. The cliff faces south and is at low elevation, so has an extended climbing season. Flagging tape on the north side of the road marks a short trail that leads through the trees to the hillside below the crag. Head more or less straight up the hillside to the base of the crag (about 30 minutes from parking).

Curbside Crags: Continue 100 m along the road past the approach trail to Silver-Tongued Devil Crag. Follow the flagging and turn right at a skull in a dead tree for Sheepshead Buttress (3 minutes). Watch for loose rock in the yellow band at the top of these routes. Follow the base of the cliffs about 100 m left (west) to reach The Monolith.

Bastion Wall: From the end of the access road (as above), cross the river and follow an old road past a meadow. Continue uphill along the road. Leave the road just before the top of the final steep section and head up a ridge, which is partially open at first and more wooded higher up. This approach reaches Bastion Wall just left of the prominent corner line of *Thor*.

Alberta Jam and ***Sunset Boulevard*:** These climbs are two of the most compelling lines in Alberta, but they are **not** sport climbs! To reach them, walk upstream (west) for about 25 minutes from the parking lot at the end of the road. *Alberta Jam* is located on a cracked, steeply inclined bedding plane atop the steep scree slope to the north (right) (see photo p. 268). Ten minutes upstream from here, but on the opposite side of the river, is the unmistakable, elegant, curving dihedral of *Sunset Boulevard* (see photo p. 269).

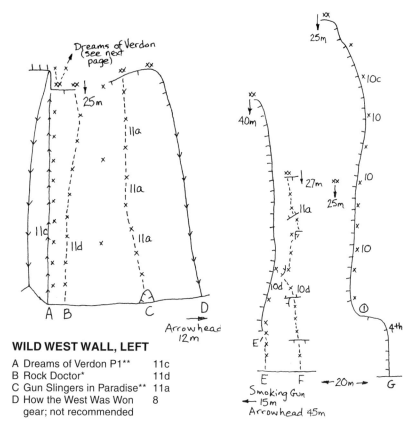

Dreams of Verdon (see next page)

25m

11a
11a
11a
11c
11d

A B   C   D

Arrowhead
12m

WILD WEST WALL, LEFT

A Dreams of Verdon P1**   11c
B Rock Doctor*   11d
C Gun Slingers in Paradise**   11a
D How the West Was Won   8
   gear; not recommended

40m

27m

11a
f

10d   10d

E

E   F

Smoking Gun
← 15m
Arrowhead 45m

25m

10c
10
10
10
10

①

4th

←20m→

G

WILD WEST WALL, RIGHT

E Cowboys Don't Cry   10d   gear to 2.5"
F Back in the Saddle**   11a
G Snerty & Me**   10c

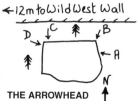

←12m to Wild West Wall

D   C   B

A

N

THE ARROWHEAD

THE ARROWHEAD

A   Solar Winds**   12b   9QDs
B   Blade Runner**   12a   9QDs
C   Vision Quest**   11d   8QDs
D   Hi Ho Silver**   10d   9QDs

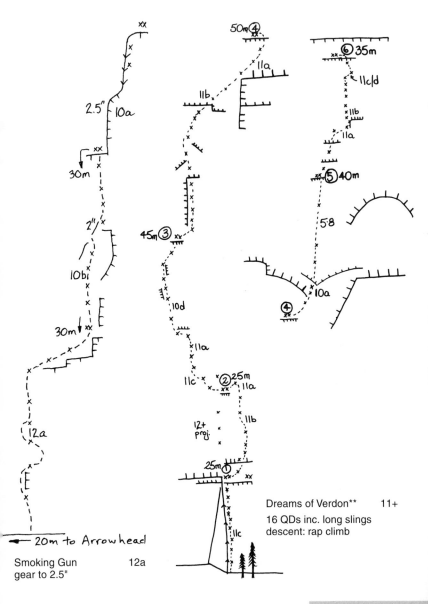

xx

50m ④

11a

11b

2.5" 10a

xx

30m

2"

10b

30m xx

12a

← 20m to Arrowhead

Smoking Gun   12a
gear to 2.5"

45m ③ xx

10d

11a

11c ② 25m
11a

12+
proj.

11b

25m ①

11c

xx ⑥ 35m

11c/d

11b

11a

xx ⑤ 40m

5·8

10a

④

Dreams of Verdon**   11+

16 QDs inc. long slings
descent: rap climb

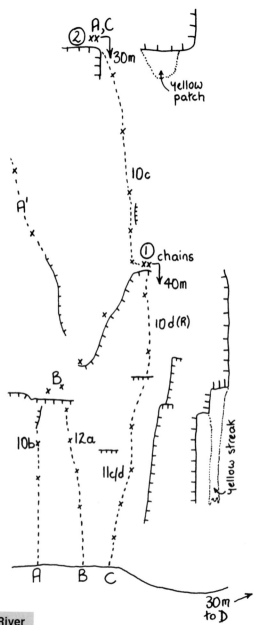

KEMP SHIELD

A	Big Rock Traditional	10c	
A'	project		
B	Shred*	12a	
C	Fool's Gold**	11c/d	
D	Cryin' Mercy**	11a/b	
E	Scaremonger*	10cR	small-med. nuts, TCUs
F	Tradesman's Entrance	8	
G	User Friendly	9	med.-large nuts
H	Boldly Go	10c/d	small nuts

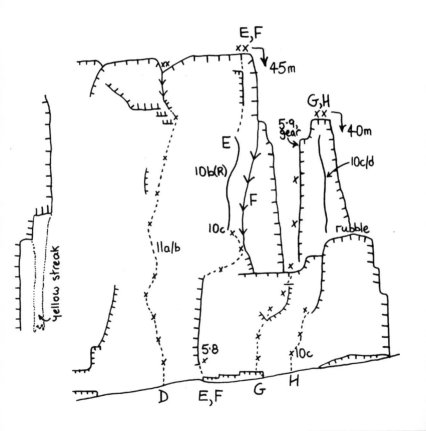

Tim Mooney on Naked teenage Girls (12a),
Barrier (p. 275). Photo Richard Akitt.

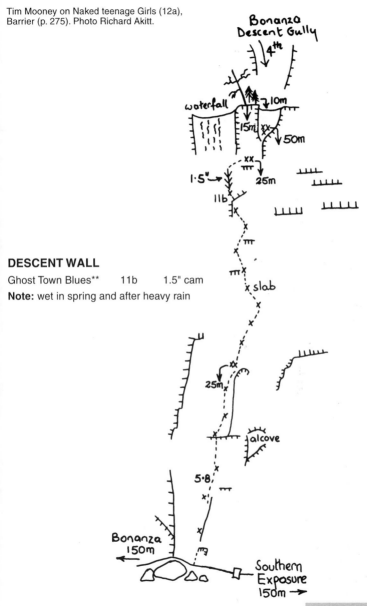

DESCENT WALL

Ghost Town Blues**   11b   1.5" cam

Note: wet in spring and after heavy rain

GREY GHOST WALL

Southern Exposure** 11a
nuts, Friends 1.5-3 (dbl #2), 12 QDs

Note: *Windmills of the Mind*
(W.M.) crosses this route
at the 2nd stance.

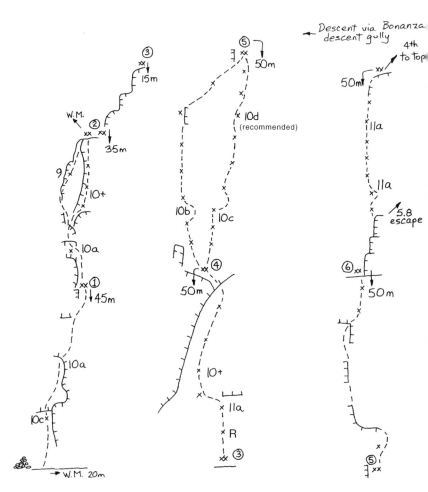

GREY GHOST WALL

Windmills of the Mind** 11b
12QDs, gear to 3", TCUs

Note: this route crosses *Southern Exposure* (S.E.) at the 2nd stance.

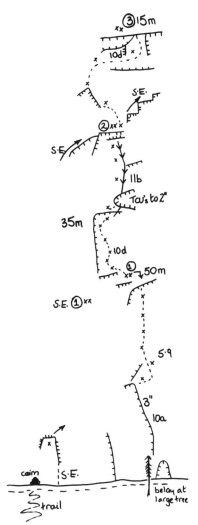

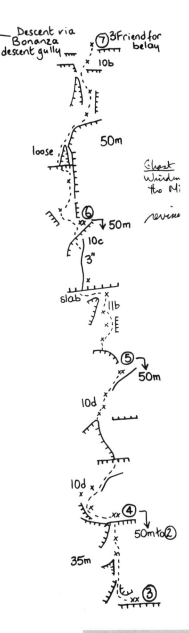

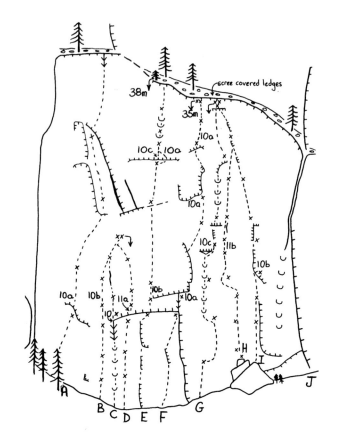

BORDERLINE BUTTRESS, LEFT

A	Travellin' Light	10b	nuts
B	Achilles**	10b	
C	Old Style*	10b	med. nuts
D	Strongbow*	11a	
E	On the Border**	10b	nuts
F	Revelations**	10a	nuts
G	Chimera**	10cR	nuts, TCUs
H	Diawl**	11b	
I	Rhydd*	10b	
J	Check Point	6	gear to 4"; not recommended

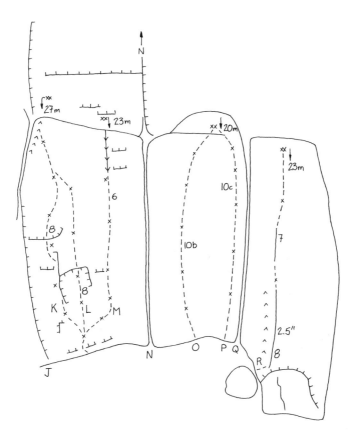

BORDERLINE BUTTRESS, RIGHT

J	Check Point	6	gear to 4"; not recommended
K	Cathedral Steps**	8	
L	Tuesday Afternoon*	8	
M	Border Rat**	6	
N	Bandidos	6	75 m; gear; not recommended
O	Legal Alien**	10b	
P	Border Sweep*	10c	
Q	Rat Patrol	7	gear; not recommended
R	Rackless*	8	gear to 2.5"

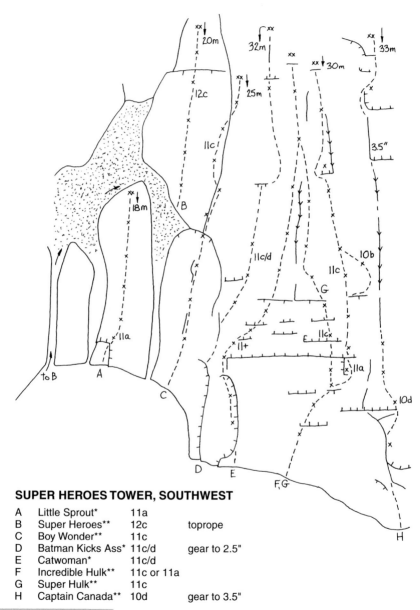

SUPER HEROES TOWER, SOUTHWEST

A	Little Sprout*	11a	
B	Super Heroes**	12c	toprope
C	Boy Wonder**	11c	
D	Batman Kicks Ass*	11c/d	gear to 2.5"
E	Catwoman*	11c/d	
F	Incredible Hulk**	11c or 11a	
G	Super Hulk**	11c	
H	Captain Canada**	10d	gear to 3.5"

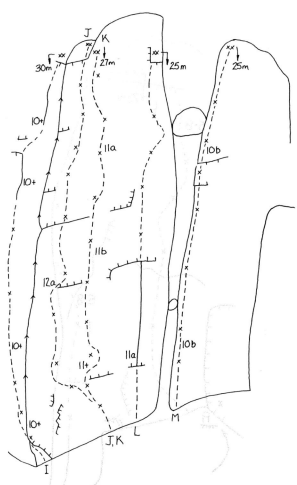

SUPER HEROES TOWER, SOUTHEAST

I   Cling of the Spiderman**   10c/d   gear to 3"
J   Superwoman's Wildest Dream**   12a
K   Flash Gordon**   11c/d
L   Wanna Fly Like Superman**   11a   gear to 2"
M   Popeye**   10b

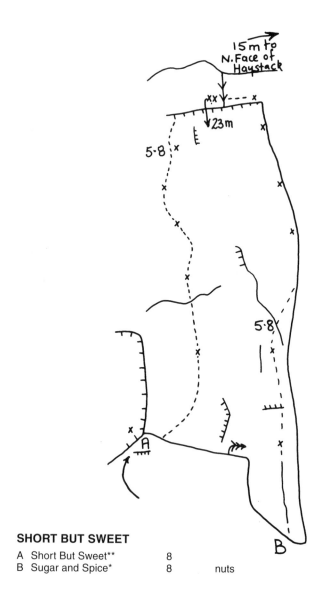

15 m to
N. Face of
Haystack

23 m

5·8

5·8

SHORT BUT SWEET

A Short But Sweet**   8
B Sugar and Spice*   8   nuts

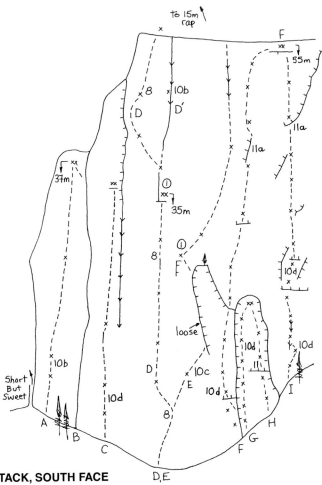

THE HAYSTACK, SOUTH FACE

A	Solitaire*	10b	nuts, TCUs
B	The Grooves*	7	gear to 2.5"
C	Midlife Crisis*	10d	nuts, RPs
D	Teenage Wasteland**	9R	nuts, RPs, #2 Friend
D'	Wasted*	10b	nuts
E	Waste of Time	10cR	nuts; not recommended
F	Heart Stopper**	11a	
G	Tower Power*	10d	
H	Quick Fling*	11b/c	
I	Lord of the Flies**	11a	

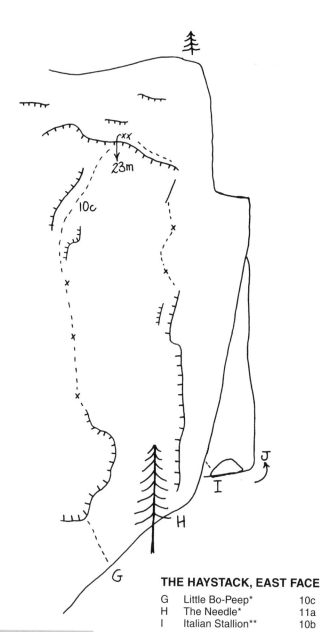

THE HAYSTACK, EAST FACE

G	Little Bo-Peep*	10c	gear to 2.5"
H	The Needle*	11a	nuts, TCUs
I	Italian Stallion**	10b	nuts

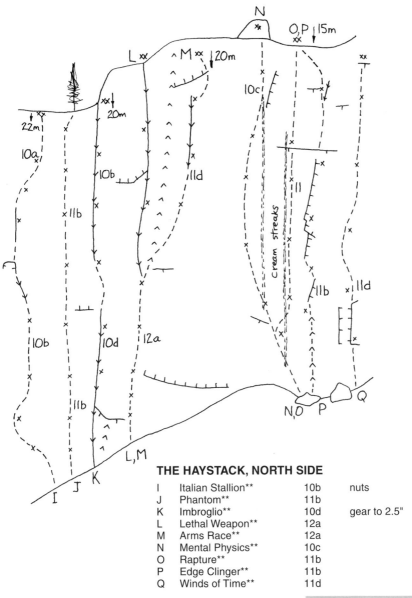

THE HAYSTACK, NORTH SIDE

I	Italian Stallion**	10b	nuts
J	Phantom**	11b	
K	Imbroglio**	10d	gear to 2.5"
L	Lethal Weapon**	12a	
M	Arms Race**	12a	
N	Mental Physics**	10c	
O	Rapture**	11b	
P	Edge Clinger**	11b	
Q	Winds of Time**	11d	

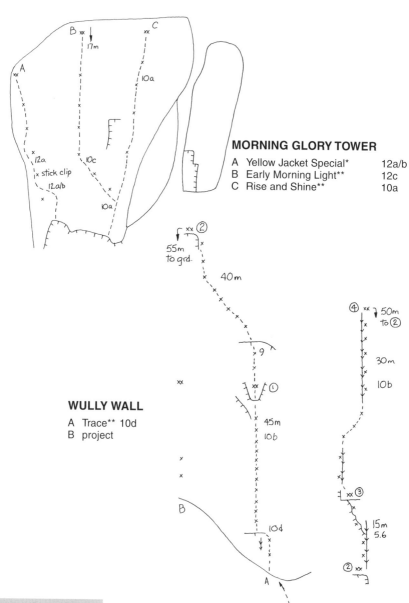

MORNING GLORY TOWER

A Yellow Jacket Special*   12a/b
B Early Morning Light**   12c
C Rise and Shine**   10a

WULLY WALL

A Trace** 10d
B project

Square Buttress. Rectangular formation in front of the main wall of *Dirty Dancing* area.

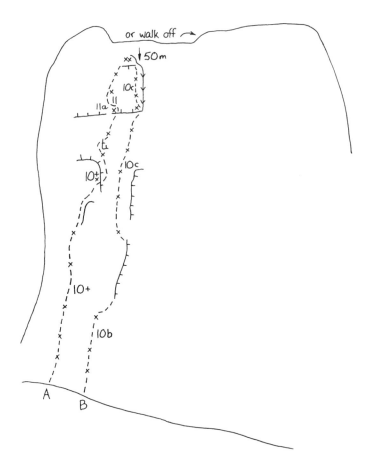

SQUARE BUTTRESS

A	Square Dance**	11a/b	med. wires
B	Hoe Down**	10c	gear to 2.5" incl. TCUs

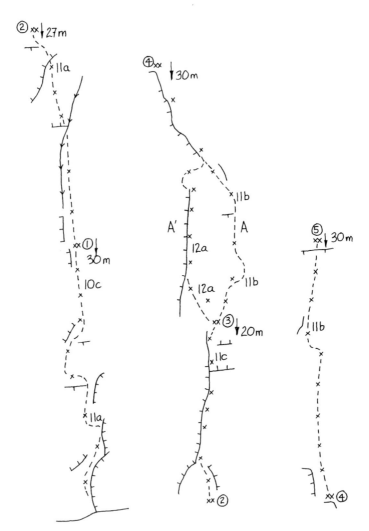

30 m right of *Dirty Dancing*.

NORTH PHANTOM CRAG

A Smokin' in the Boys Room** 11c
A' Ghost Dance**   12a

10 m right of *Smokin' in the Boys Room*.

NORTH PHANTOM CRAG

A Don't Forget to Dance**   11d
B Be My Partner**   10c

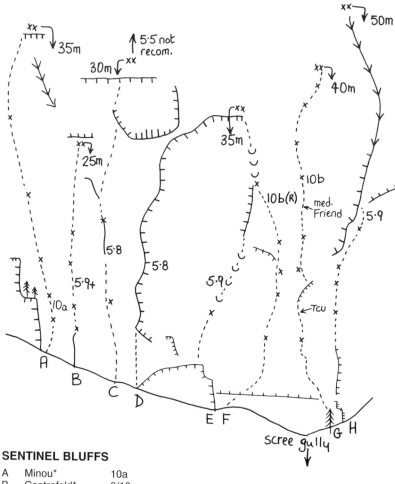

SENTINEL BLUFFS

A	Minou*	10a	
B	Centrefold*	9/10a	
C	Pin-Up	8	nuts, Friends, RPs
D	Black Mango	8	nuts
E	Creeping Senility	9	nuts
F	Softly Softly**	10bR	nuts
G	Twinkle Toes**	10b	nuts, TCUs, med. Friend
H	Feeling Groovy	9	nuts, TCUs

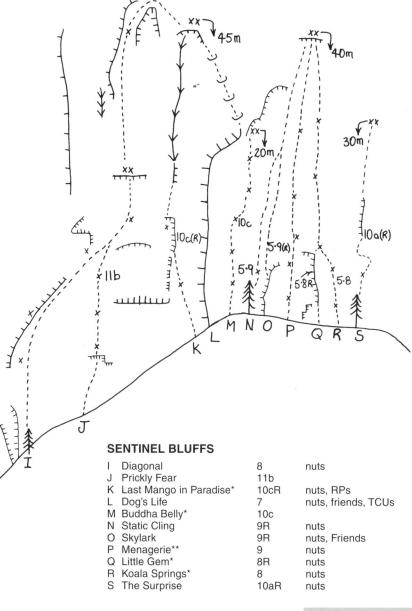

SENTINEL BLUFFS

I	Diagonal	8	nuts
J	Prickly Fear	11b	
K	Last Mango in Paradise*	10cR	nuts, RPs
L	Dog's Life	7	nuts, friends, TCUs
M	Buddha Belly*	10c	
N	Static Cling	9R	nuts
O	Skylark	9R	nuts, Friends
P	Menagerie**	9	nuts
Q	Little Gem*	8R	nuts
R	Koala Springs*	8	nuts
S	The Surprise	10aR	nuts

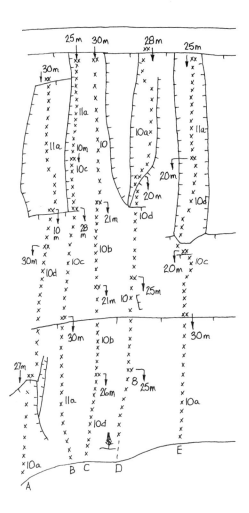

SILVER-TONGUED DEVIL CRAG

A Essence*   10a, 10d, 11a
B Seducin' Medusa**   11a, 10c, 10c, 11a
C Southern Lines**   10d, 10b, 10b, 10b
D Grindstone*   8, 10a, 10d, 10a
E Summerteeth**   10a, 10c, 10d, 11a
F Talk-Action=0**   9, 10c, 10a, 11a
G Jerkin'a Gherkin*   10b, 10b, 10d, 10a

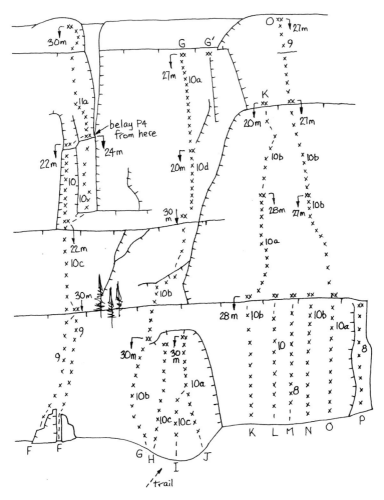

G' project
H Seams Easy*   10c
I Report a Poacher   10c
J Slabulous*   10a
K Up in Arms**   10b, 10a, 10b
L Mom's Time Out*   10b
M Ghosts of Phyl and George*   8
N This Bolt's for You*   10b
O Heidies with Hilties*   10a, 10b, 10b, 9
P Weird Tales*   8

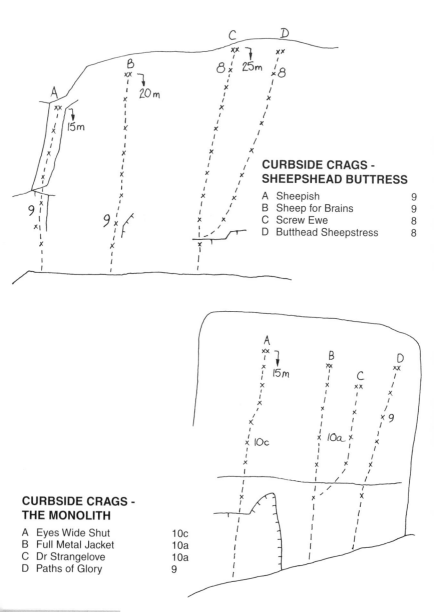

**CURBSIDE CRAGS –
SHEEPSHEAD BUTTRESS**

A Sheepish — 9
B Sheep for Brains — 9
C Screw Ewe — 8
D Butthead Sheepstress — 8

**CURBSIDE CRAGS –
THE MONOLITH**

A Eyes Wide Shut — 10c
B Full Metal Jacket — 10a
C Dr Strangelove — 10a
D Paths of Glory — 9

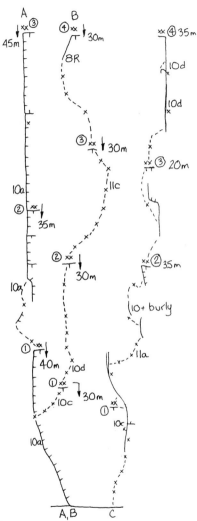

BASTION WALL

A	Thor**	10a	gear to 3"
B	Men of Fashion**	11c/d	gear to 3" (P1 only)
C	The Curio Emporium**	11a	gear to 3.5"; 2 ropes for P2 (traverse to B to descend)

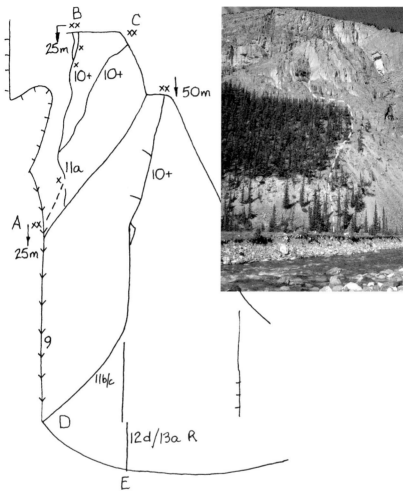

ALBERTA JAM

A	Recky Route**	9	gear to 4"
B	Fat City**	11a	gear to 3.5"
C	October Finger Fest**	11a	gear to 2"
D	Alberta Jam**	11b/c	gear to 3.5"
E	Dionysus**	12d/13aR	gear to 3.5", many RPs

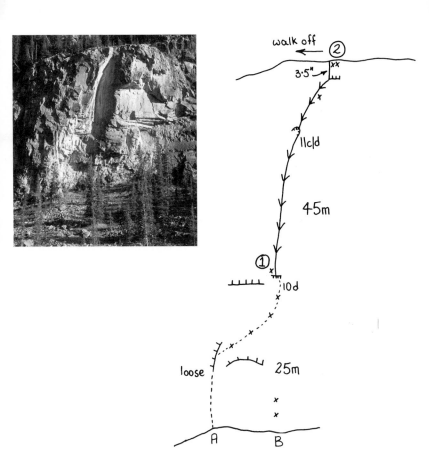

walk off ←

② xx

3.5"

x

11c|d

45m

① x

10d

x

x

x

loose

25m

x

x

A   B

SUNSET BOULEVARD

A Sunset Boulevard**   11c/d   gear to 3.5", RPs
B project (abandoned)

BARRIER MOUNTAIN

The main climbing area at Barrier Mountain is a long cliff on the north and northwest sides of the mountain, near the highway. The area left of "L" in the photo has numerous traditional rock climbs, covered in Kelly Tobey's guidebook *Barrier Bluffs – the Guide*.

Approach

Park in the ditch on the eastbound side of the highway near a road sign about 150 m east of the crest of a big hill northwest of the mountain. The access trail is clearly visible leading up the grass of the highway cut slope. After a short section through the woods, the trail follows a major gully. Spur trails lead left to Lumpy Corner, Escape Wall and Yellow Wall, any of which can be reached in about 15 minutes from the road. To reach Squid Crack, continue up the gully trail past the end of Yellow Wall for about 10 minutes until the gully opens out. Leave the gully and angle slightly left up through trees to a cliff band—Squid Crack. Follow the cliff band left to get to Middle Earth. To get to Upper Barrier, follow the trail to the top of the gully and then a short distance left (about 45 minutes from the road). Slogger's Dream Wall is beyond the end of the trail, about 15 minutes farther along. To reach Salt & Pepper, find a trail leaving the road about 50 m east of the main access trail. Follow it to the cliffs near the junction of the north and west facing walls, then continue east (left) along the base of the cliff. Look for a pockmarked slab (visible from the highway).

E Escape Wall,   Y Yellow Wall,   M Middle Earth,   Q Squid Crack,   U Upper Barrier,   S Slogger's Dream Wall,   L Lumpy Corner, P Salt & Pepper

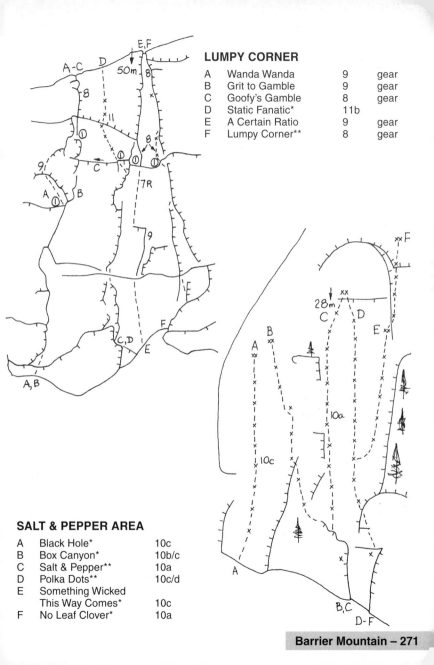

LUMPY CORNER

A	Wanda Wanda	9	gear
B	Grit to Gamble	9	gear
C	Goofy's Gamble	8	gear
D	Static Fanatic*	11b	
E	A Certain Ratio	9	gear
F	Lumpy Corner**	8	gear

SALT & PEPPER AREA

A	Black Hole*	10c
B	Box Canyon*	10b/c
C	Salt & Pepper**	10a
D	Polka Dots**	10c/d
E	Something Wicked This Way Comes*	10c
F	No Leaf Clover*	10a

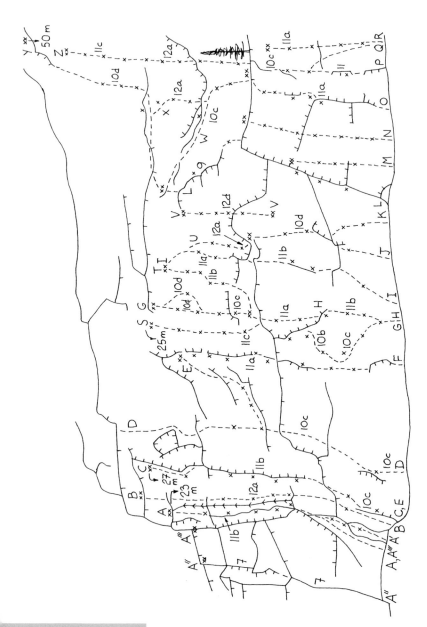

272 – Barrier Mountain

ESCAPE WALL

A	Koyaanisqatsi**	11b	
A'	Koyaanisqatsi Direct	11a	
A''	Lockin' 'r Hookin'***	7	gear
A'''	Drifter's Escape	9	offwidth gear
B	Double Clutch**	12a	
C	Ideal for Living**	11b	Rock 5
D	2 + 2 = 5	10c	not recommended
E	Brazilian Buzz*	10a	
F	The Great Outdoors*	11a	
G	A.K.A.**	10d	
H	Channel Zero	11b	
I	Through a Glass Darkly*	11b	wired nuts, #0 Slider
J	The Roman Empire	10d	
K	M.E.C.	10d	
L	Nuts of Steel	10a	
M	Sensoria**	12a	
N	Kiwis Fly	12d	
O	Cost of Living**	11a	
P	Age of Reason Direct	11c	
Q	Age of Reason*	10c	
R	Blank on the Map*	11a	
S	Bango	11c	
T	Winnebago Warrior**	11b	
U	Scribble Feet	12a*	
V	Fries and Gravy	12d	
W	Sharky's Revenge	10c	
X	Where's Your Child?	12a	
Y	Tempted to Exist	10d	
Z	Requiem*	12a	

YELLOW WALL

P	Age of Reason Direct	11c	
Q	Age of Reason*	10c	
R	Blank on the Map*	11a	
Z	Requiem*	12a	
AA	Hollow Men*	10b	
BB	I Drill Therefore I Am	10c	
CC	Shadow Play	10a	
DD	Untitled	9	
EE	One Way to Wangland*	8	
FF	Current Account*	10a	
GG	Front Row Centre*	7	
HH	Serial Driller*	9	
II	Raindance*	9	
JJ	There Goes the Neighbourhood*	9	
KK	Drill of a Lifetime**	9	
LL	Cadillac Jack*	9	
MM	Squeeze Play	10d	
NN	The Wasp*	9	
OO	End Dance*	10c	
PP	Iron in the Soul*	11a	nuts to Rock 8, Friend 2
QQ	Regatta de Blank	12b	
RR	Naked Teenage Girls*	12a	
SS	Rainbow Bridge*	10b	Rock 6 or 7, long sling
TT	Sisyphus Goes to Hollywood**	11c	
UU	In Us Under Us**	11b	
VV	The Flake*	11a	small wired nuts
WW	Feel Surreal	11b	

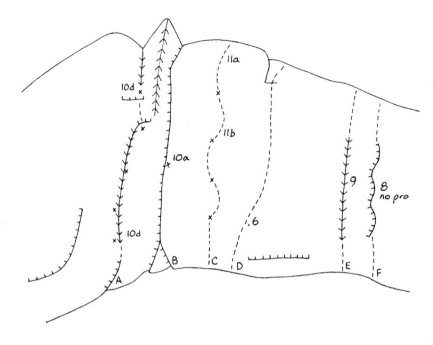

SQUID CRACK

A	Moe and Larry Go to France	10d	
B	Squid Crack*	10a	TCUs to Friend 3
C	The Trial*	11b	
D	Unnamed	6	no pro
E	Weasel	8	TCUs, Friend 1.5
F	Squirrel	6	no pro

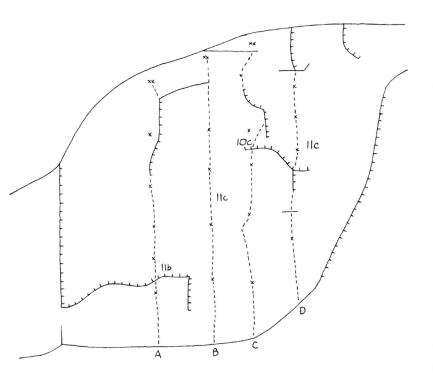

MIDDLE EARTH

A Surf the Earth*   11b
B Grasping at the Wind*   11c
C Throbbing Gristle*   10c
D Wild Turkey Surprise   11c

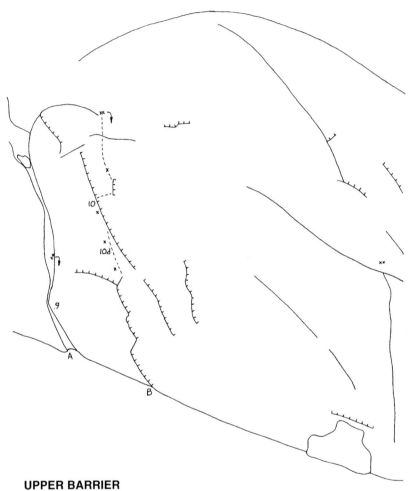

UPPER BARRIER

A Big Crack Attack	9	gear to Friend 4
B Big Dark Dreams*	10d	
To Tame a Land	A2	(crack around corner to left)

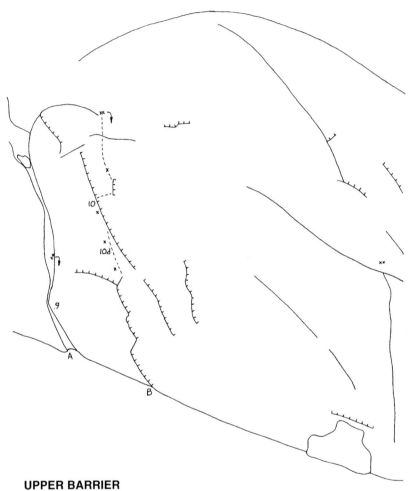

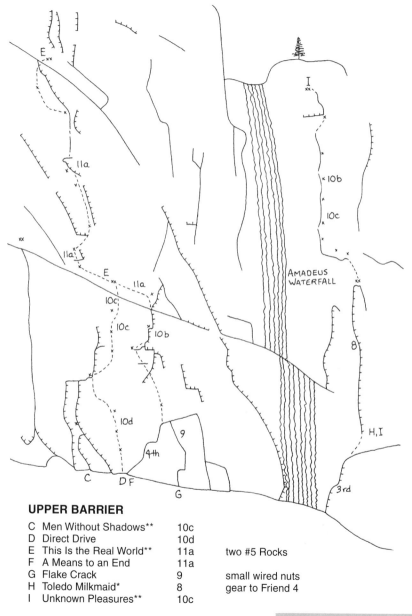

UPPER BARRIER

C	Men Without Shadows**	10c	
D	Direct Drive	10d	
E	This Is the Real World**	11a	two #5 Rocks
F	A Means to an End	11a	
G	Flake Crack	9	small wired nuts
H	Toledo Milkmaid*	8	gear to Friend 4
I	Unknown Pleasures**	10c	

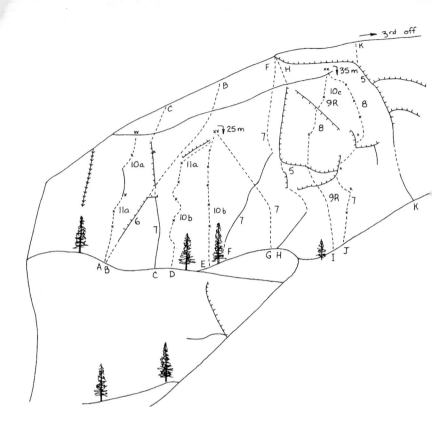

SLOGGER'S DREAM WALL

A	Charisma**	11a	small wired nuts
B	Escape from Nap Town	6	gear to 2.5"
C	Yah Weh Up There*	7	gear to 3"
D	The Longest Yard	11a	
E	Albedo**	10b	
F	Breezeway	7	small nuts
G	Crossfire	7	no pro
H	Pie in the Sky	5	gear to 2.5"
I	Point Blank	10c	RP2
J	Maid to Measure**	8	
K	Walk in Light	5	gear to 2"

PORCUPINE CREEK

Several small climbing areas have been established in the valley of Porcupine Creek. All the cliffs face south or southwest and get plenty of sun.

Approach
Park on the highway shoulder (off the pavement) near the creek crossing. Follow a gravel track on the left side of the creek until it peters out near the first bend in the valley, then continue along sketchy trails near the creek. Hyperion, a small slab, is just around the first bend, about 10 - 15 minutes from the highway. Blind Man's Bluff, a long, low, steep cliff, is a short distance farther. No creek crossings are required to this point. Just beyond Blind Man's Bluff the creek forks; follow the left fork for about 15 minutes to get to The Hedgehog, a steep slab. Uphill from The Hedgehog are two more slabs: Prickly Heat (5 minutes) and Further to Fly (10 minutes).

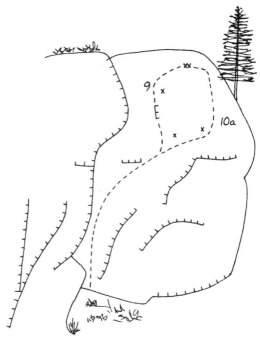

HYPERION

A	Hyperion Left	9	Friends 1 & 2
B	Hyperion Right	10a	Friend 1

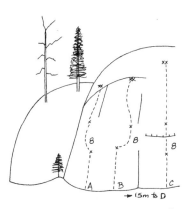

BLIND MAN'S BLUFF

A	Prickly Pear	8
B	The Porcupine Climb	8
C	Short But Small	8

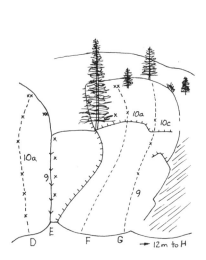

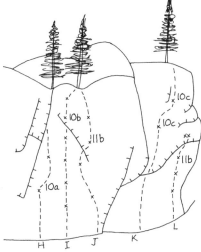

D	Shortcut	10a	
E	unnamed	9	
F	Small But Short	10a	
G	Blind Man's Bluff	10c	
H	Snowblind*	10a	medium Friend
I	Blind Date**	10b	
J	Blind Alley*	11b	
K	Surf's Up*	10c	nuts, Friend 1.5
L	Under the Weather*	11b	

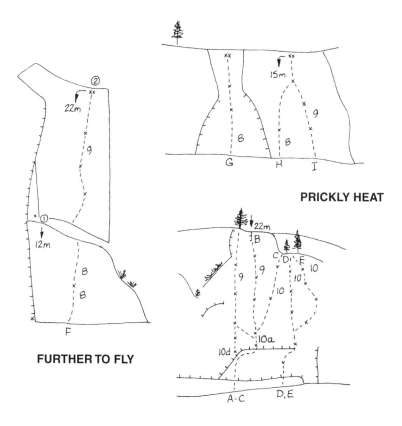

PRICKLY HEAT

FURTHER TO FLY

THE HEDGEHOG

A	Reclining Porcupine*	10a or 10d	
B	Repining Porcuclimb*	10a	
C	Hystrix*	10a	small wired nuts
D	Prickles**	10c	
E	Spiny Norman*	10b	
F	Further to Fly	9	
G	Lead on McPhail	8	
H	Prickly Heat	8	
I	Can't Stand to Drill	9	

This is a set of southwest-facing slabs in the valley of Wasootch Creek. The short approach, favourable sun exposure and large number of climbs available at moderate standards combine to make crowds common here, especially in spring. Wasootch is traditionally a toprope area, but there are some good lead routes too. Rockfall hazard is high—**ALWAYS WEAR A HELMET**.

A major renovation of Wasootch Slabs was initiated by TABVAR in 2001. Its purpose is to improve safety by providing additional lead routes and adding protection to existing ones (to reduce the need to scramble to the top of the cliffs to set up topropes), adding new toprope anchors and moving others to better locations, segregating lead and toprope areas, and decommissioning routes that constitute a safety hazard due to loose rock. Renovation work has been completed in some priority areas and this edition of the guidebook reflects the changes completed by the end of 2001. D, E and G Slabs as shown here are essentially complete but additional work is planned for all the other slabs up to "F". As changes are made they will be posted to the TABVAR pages under Links at www.strongholdclimbing.com.

The new top anchors at Wasootch are doubled ring anchors. While sturdy, they can wear out with over-use. Therefore, please toprope off these anchors using your own gear (i.e. use quickdraws or a sling and carabiners; last person up retrieves the gear and lowers or raps off the anchors.)

Approach

Turn south from Highway 40 to reach the Wasootch Creek parking area. The turn-off is signed. The first climbing areas are 5 minutes' walk up the valley. Years ago, the Canadian Army (which holds annual training courses here) identified the main climbing rocks by large painted letters from A to G, starting at the north. Four less well-known rocks lie about 10 minutes' walk beyond G Slab, just past the first bend in the valley. Irish Rock is the first cliff past the bend; Y Slab and Four Pines are a little farther along, past a steep yellow wall; and tiny Z Slab, almost hidden by trees, is the last outcrop on the left as the valley widens out, about 75 m beyond Four Pines.

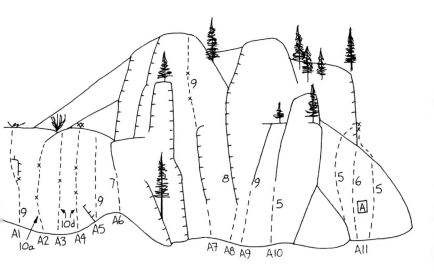

A SLAB

A1	The Eggplant That Ate Chicago*	9	small wired nut
A2	Return of Eggplant	10a	
A3	The Eggplant's Revenge	10d	
A4	Attack of the Killer Tomatoes	10d	
A5	Son of Eggplant	9	no pro
A6		7	gear
A7	Fossil Wall*	9	small wired nuts
A8	Takes Balls Instead	8	poor pro
A9		9	small nuts
A10		5	gear
A11		5 or 6	toprope

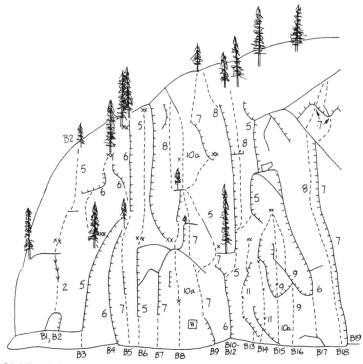

B SLAB, LEFT

B1		2	gear
B2		5	gear
B3		6	gear
B4		5	gear
B5		7	gear
B6		5	gear
B7		7	gear
B8	Stumped	10a	
B9	B-line	8 or 10a	many small nuts
B10	The Funnel*	8	gear
B11	Funnel Arête	8	RPs
B12		6	gear
B13	Smoke on the Water	11b	
B14	Machine Head*	11a	
B15	Arborist	10a	minimal pro
B16	Poplar Mechanics	9	nuts, Friend 4
B17	First Corner	7	gear
B18	Orange Arête	8	wired nuts
B19	Second Corner*	7	gear

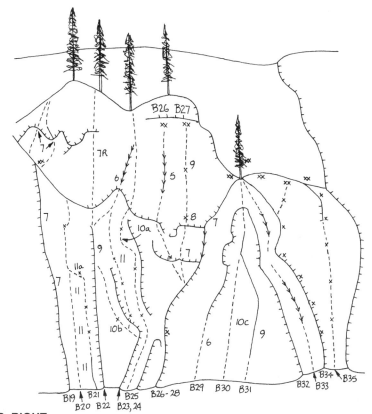

B SLAB, RIGHT

B20	Stiletto	11d	toprope
B21	Wall Street*	11a	small nut
B22	Third Corner**	9	Friends
B23	Exhibit A*	10b	gear
B24	Exhibit B	11	
B25	Silver Bullet**	10a	small wired nut
B26	Good Gear*	7	gear
B27	Cracked Slab**	9	gear
B28	Steps Pinnacle, Far Left	7	toprope
B29	Steps Pinnacle, Left	7	toprope
B30	Mama Said	10c	toprope
B31	Steps Crack	9	toprope
B32	Steps Pinnacle, Regular*	7	toprope
B33	Steps Pinnacle, Right*	7	toprope
B34	Steps Pinnacle, Far Right	6	
B35		6	

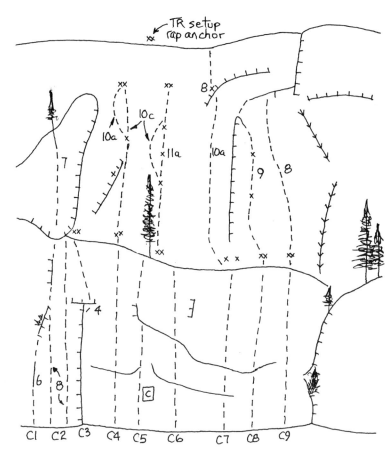

C SLAB, LEFT

C1		7	gear
C2		8	toprope
C3		4	gear
C4		10a or 10c	
C5	Sweet Tweet*	10c or 11a	
C6		4	toprope
C7	Flakes Away	10a	
C8	Pancake, Direct	9	toprope
C9	Pancake, Centre	8	no pro

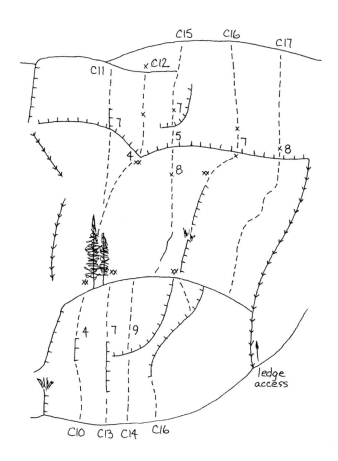

C SLAB, RIGHT

C10		4	toprope
C11	C Roof, Left	7	gear
C12	C Roof, Regular*	4	gear
C13		7	toprope
C14		9	toprope
C15	C Roof, Near Right	8	
C16	C Roof, Right	7	
C17	C Roof, Far Right	8	

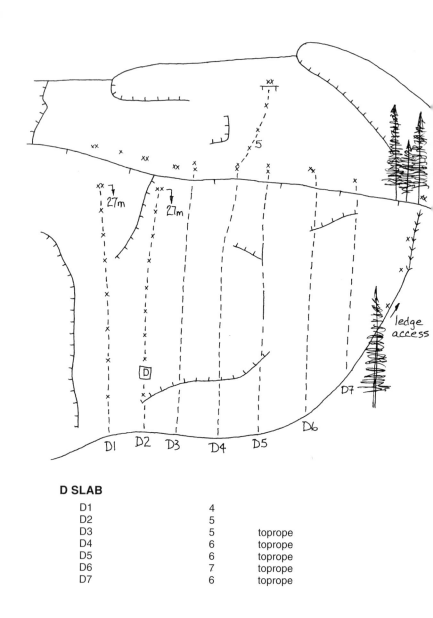

D SLAB

D1	4	
D2	5	
D3	5	toprope
D4	6	toprope
D5	6	toprope
D6	7	toprope
D7	6	toprope

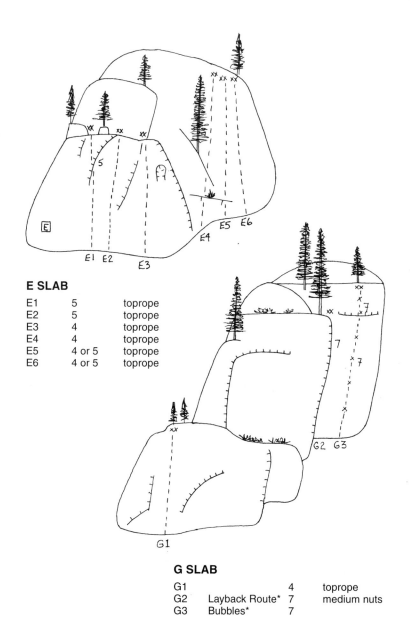

E SLAB

E1	5	toprope
E2	5	toprope
E3	4	toprope
E4	4	toprope
E5	4 or 5	toprope
E6	4 or 5	toprope

G SLAB

G1		4	toprope
G2	Layback Route*	7	medium nuts
G3	Bubbles*	7	

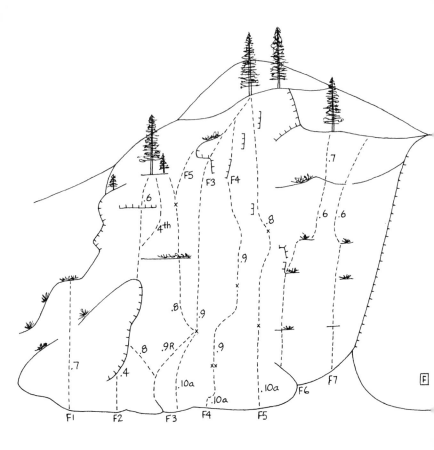

F SLAB

F1		7	no pro
F2		4 or 6	gear
F3	Moon Unit	9R or 10a	small wired nuts
F4	Nasty Habits*	10a	wired nuts
F5	Locomotion*	9 or 10a	wired nuts
F6		7	poor pro
F7		6	poor pro

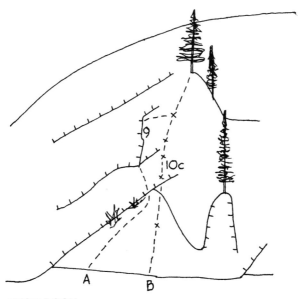

IRISH ROCK

A	Canadian Debut	9	not recommended
B	Ozada*	10c	

Z SLAB

Z1	Burger Time	9
Z2	Slot Machine*	10a
Z3	Reverse English	10b
Z4	Aristocrat*	10d
Z5	Body Language	10b

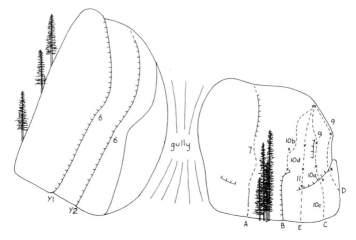

Y SLAB

Y1	6	no pro
Y2	6	no pro

FOUR PINES

A	Rubby's Route	7	Friends
B	Synchrotron*	10d	Friend 1
C	Stone Talk*	10c	
D	Shrinking Violet*	9	
E	Subvert the Dominant Paradigm	11	

Mount Lorette, showing Lorette Slab.

LORETTE SLAB

This is a west-facing, highly textured bedding plane slab located in the major gully on the south side of Mount Lorette. The climbs are of the friction/face variety and may seem somewhat runout by modern standards.

Approach
Starting at Ribbon Creek, bike the powerline trail north and then east as far as a sharp drop-off at the foot of Mount Lorette. Park your bike and follow a faint trail left into the gully. Climb up the gully until a clean slab can be seen a short distance up the slope on the east (right) side. This is Lorette Slab. To approach, detour some intervening slabs on their left side. On the way down it is easier to traverse south from the base of Lorette Slab and descend scree to the gully. The approach takes about an hour from Ribbon Creek. Don't try fording the Kananaskis River to save time—the river is controlled for power generation and may be too deep to cross when you return.

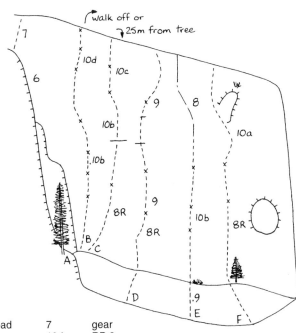

A	Reading Railroad	7	gear
B	Nineveh**	10d	RP 3
C	Boardwalk*	10c	RP 2
D	Atlantic Avenue*	9	RP 2
E	Park Place*	10b	small wired nuts
F	Marvin Gardens	10a	RP 2

This is a small, west-facing, slabby cliff south of Highway 40 near a microwave tower at the base of a prominent gully. Small edges rule and protection is a bit sparse.

Approach
Take a dirt turnoff 1.4 km southwest of Wasootch Creek to a large open area. Walk up the hill to a gravel road near the microwave tower. Turn left, walk along the road a short distance, and then go directly up to the crag—about 15 minutes from the highway.

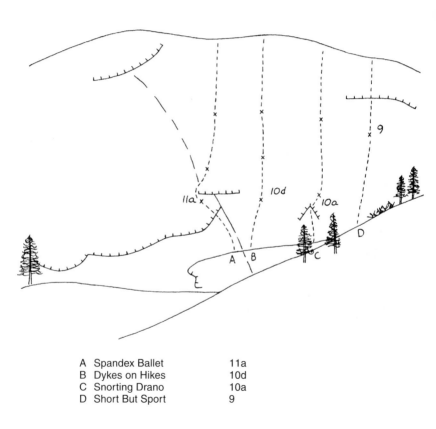

A	Spandex Ballet	11a
B	Dykes on Hikes	10d
C	Snorting Drano	10a
D	Short But Sport	9

MCDOUGALL SLABS

This friction climbing area is on the west side of Mount McDougall's northernmost peak, across the Kananaskis Valley from Nakiska. Get here early if you want to do the harder climbs—they become slippery on warm afternoons. Protection is sparse by modern standards but not unreasonable. Take 2 ropes except for Little McDougall Slab.

Approach
Park at the Mount Allan (Nakiska) pull-out on Highway 40, 2.6 km south of Wasootch Creek. Cross the highway and find a narrow trail leading into the woods. This trail will take you to Little McDougall Slab in 30 - 40 minutes. Big McDougall Slab is 2 - 3 minutes farther up the trail. Aldebaran is reached from Big McDougall by following the base of the slabs up and right about 10 minutes to a gully. Scramble up and left from the base of Aldebaran to reach Pellucidar. Capella is up and right from the top of Aldebaran.

L Little McDougall,　B Big McDougall,　A Aldebaran,　P Pellucidar,　C Capella

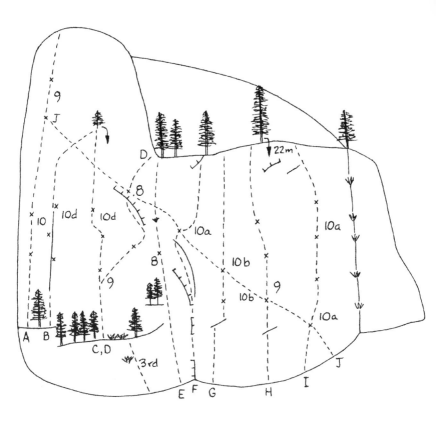

LITTLE MCDOUGALL SLAB

A	Lube Job*	10c
B	Groover**	10d
C	Sole Survivor*	10d
D	Replay	9	medium nut
E	Botany Bay	8	medium nut
F	Reflex	10a
G	Greaser*	10b
H	Scarface*	9
I	Fluvial Foont**	10a
J	One Hour Martinizing*	10b

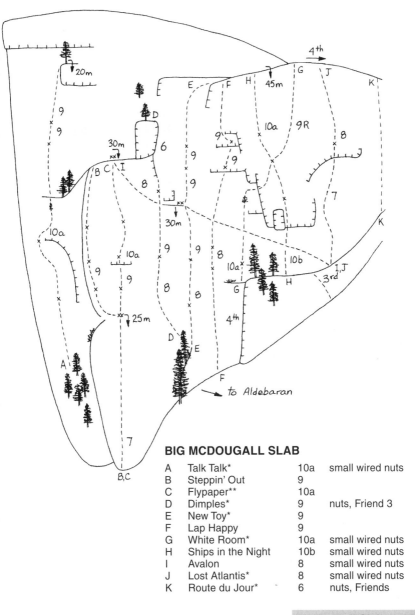

BIG MCDOUGALL SLAB

A	Talk Talk*	10a	small wired nuts
B	Steppin' Out	9	
C	Flypaper**	10a	
D	Dimples*	9	nuts, Friend 3
E	New Toy*	9	
F	Lap Happy	9	
G	White Room*	10a	small wired nuts
H	Ships in the Night	10b	small wired nuts
I	Avalon	8	small wired nuts
J	Lost Atlantis*	8	small wired nuts
K	Route du Jour*	6	nuts, Friends

John Martin on Shibalba (10c).
Cowbell Crag (p. 305). Photo Steve Stahl.

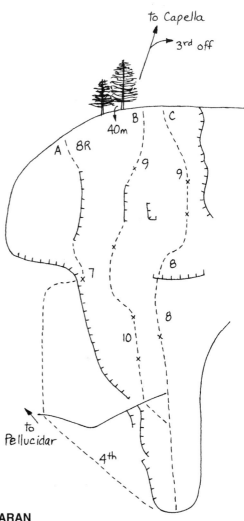

ALDEBARAN

A	Gemini 11	8	small wired nuts
B	Arcturus	10b	
C	Aldebaran	9	Friend 2
D	Capella	10b	small wired nuts, RPs

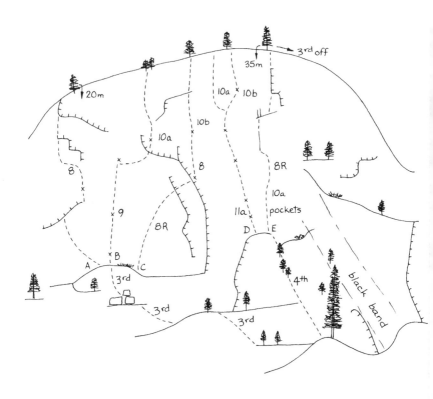

PELLUCIDAR

A	Antares	8	small wired nuts
B	Flashpoint*	10a	
C	Rimshot	10b	
D	Pellucidar*	11a	
E	Natural Lite	10a	small wired nuts, Friends

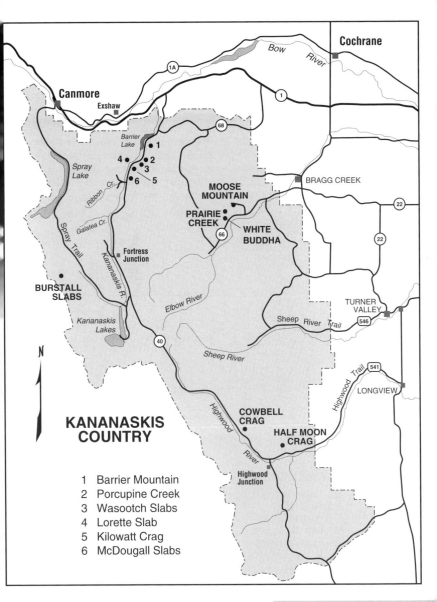

Cochrane

Bow River

Canmore

Exshaw

1A

1

Barrier Lake

Spray Lake

4

3

2

5

6

Ribbon Cr.

Galatea Cr.

68

MOOSE MOUNTAIN

PRAIRIE CREEK

WHITE BUDDHA

66

BRAGG CREEK

22

22

Spray Trail

Fortress Junction

Kananaskis R.

BURSTALL SLABS

Kananaskis Lakes

Elbow River

TURNER VALLEY

546

Sheep River Trail

40

Sheep River

Highwood Trail

541

LONGVIEW

N

KANANASKIS COUNTRY

Highwood River

COWBELL CRAG

HALF MOON CRAG

Highwood Junction

1 Barrier Mountain
2 Porcupine Creek
3 Wasootch Slabs
4 Lorette Slab
5 Kilowatt Crag
6 McDougall Slabs

Perhaps the most unusual cliff yet developed in the guidebook area, Cowbell Crag is formed by a moderately steep bedding plane of conglomerate. The cliff is characterized by numerous cracks, both vertical and horizontal, and many of the routes require a relatively extensive gear rack including RPs and TCUs. Two ropes are needed to rappel the routes, but there is an easy walk-off descent at the north end of the cliff. Cowbell Crag catches afternoon sun and is warm early and late in the year.

Approach

Cowbell Crag is on the east side of Highway 40, 9.6 km north of Highwood Junction. Park in the ditch at a cairn, which marks the start of the 2 minute approach trail. Stick to the indicated access routes to reach the climbs—other potential accesses have not been cleaned and may be dangerously loose. Highway 40 is closed at Highwood Junction between December 1 - June 15, but Cowbell Crag is easily reached from the south by bicycle as soon as the snow melts off the highway (usually early May).

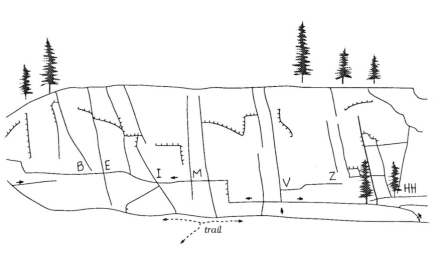

COWBELL OVERVIEW

B	Home on the Range
E	High Noon
I	Jugs for Thugs
M	Left Ski Track
V	Fags on Crags
Z	Vanishing Crack
HH	Pebbles

COWBELL CRAG, LEFT

A	Ranchman's Crack	6	gear to Friend 3
B	Home on the Range*	6	gear to Friend 3.5
C	I Wanna Be a Cowboy*	8	gear to Friend 4, TCUs
D	Hired Gun*	10a	RP 2, TCU 1 or 2, Friend 2
E	High Noon	9	gear to Friend 3
F	Boot Hill*	10d	gear to Friend 3.5
G	Lariat Crack	10c	gear to Friend 3.5
H	Guano Roof	10b	gear to Friend 3
I	Jugs for Thugs*	10a	gear to Friend 4
J	Osiris*	10b	dbl cams to Friend 2.5, RPs
K	Shibalba**	10c	Friends 0.5-2
L	Ride the River*	10b	gear to Friend 3, RPs

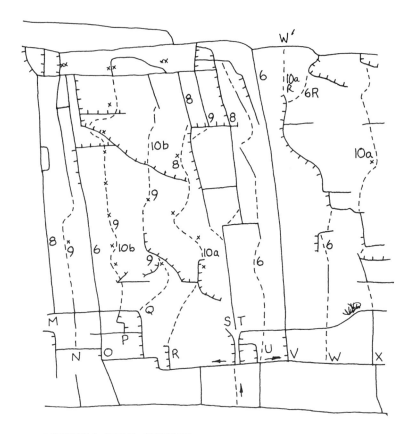

COWBELL CRAG, CENTRE

M	Left Ski Track	8	RP 4 to Friend 3
N	Inside Track*	9	cams to Friend 3.5
O	Right Ski Track	7	gear to Friend 4
P	The Last Roundup	10b	TCU 2
Q	Isis**	10b	cams to Friend 3
R	Range Wars*	10a	gear to Friend 3
S	Bunny Duck Roof*	9	gear to Friend 3
T	Animal Magnetism	8	gear to Friend 3
U	Poodle on a Leash	7	gear to 2"
V	Fags on Crags	6	gear to Friend 3
W	Domino	6R	gear to 2"
W'	Too Much Licorice	10aR	gear to 2"
X	Semi-Honed**	10a	cams to Friend 3

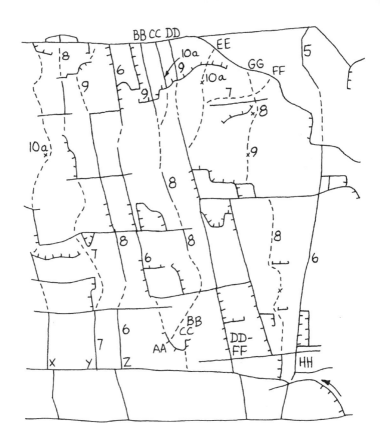

COWBELL CRAG, RIGHT

X	Semi-Honed**	10a	
Y	Mosaic	8	RP 2 to Friend 3.5
Z	Vanishing Crack**	9	gear to Friend 3.5
AA	Eugene	6	gear to Friend 4
BB	Bruno's Crack*	9	gear to Friend 3
CC	DB's Variation*	10a	RP 3 to Friend 3
DD	Secret Agent*	9	gear to Friend 3.5
EE	Abraxas	10a	gear to Friend 3.5
FF	Agent Orange	7	gear to Friend 3.5
GG	Knob Job	9	cams to Friend 2
HH	Pebbles	6	gear to Friend 3

A steep limestone slab, Half Moon Crag offers excellent, if limited, thin crack climbing. Take a full rack, including all the small gear you can rustle up. The cliff faces east and goes out of the sun in the afternoon—thus if you are chasing either sun or shade a trip here combines perfectly with a visit to nearby west-facing Cowbell Crag.

Approach

The cliff is located in a side drainage north of the Highwood Road, near Highwood Junction. Park at a small unnamed stream that descends man-made steps, 2.5 km west of Fir Creek (a marked stream crossing) and 4.4 km east of Highwood Junction. Follow a good game trail on the east side of the creek for about 20 minutes until it crosses over to the west side. Half Moon Crag is now visible on the open slopes above to the left, another 20 minutes away.

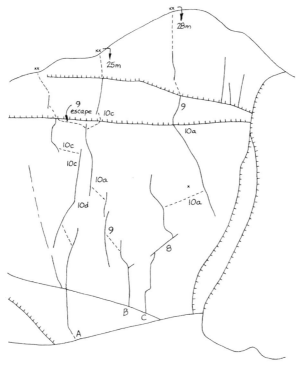

A	Eclipse**	10d	gear to Friend 2, TCUs, 2 sets RPs
B	Hunter's Moon**	10c	gear to Friend 2, TCUs, 2 sets RPs
C	Moonstruck**	10a	RPs, gear to Friend 3.5

Pam Pearson on Beat the Clock (11c/d), Bataan (p. 174).
Photo Roger Chayer, TALUS Photographics.

Here, on a series of west-facing bedding plane slabs some 200 m high, is one of North America's finest friction climbing areas, combining top quality rock, excellent climbing and an alpine setting. As friction climbs go, the harder Burstall routes are unusually steep and taxing; *Lunatic Fringe* is particularly in-your-face and should on no account be missed by slab specialists. Protection standards are consistent with or better than those on comparable cliffs such as the Glacier Point and Squamish aprons. Although there are many bolts, there are also a lot of gear placements, particularly on the easier climbs. Recommended rack: a full set of wired nuts plus RPs, TCUs and Friends. Double 50 m ropes are mandatory and we recommend wearing a helmet in case parties above you dislodge rocks from the top of the cliff or from Avens Avenue. Several fully equipped, one-pitch climbs have been established on Lunar Slab for those who wish to hone their footing technique before venturing onto the bigger routes.

In addition to the routes shown here, the North and Central gullies have both been climbed. Both are loose and not recommended.

Approach

From Mud Lake parking lot (midway between Kananaskis Lakes and Spray Lake on the Spray Lakes Road), follow the Burstall Pass trail nearly to the pass before contouring left to reach the base of the slabs: about 2 hours on foot or 1.5 hours with a bicycle. The upper part of the approach route may be snowbound until well into July; however, the southwesterly aspect of the cliff allows climbing well into October in good years. Burstall Creek must be forded at the 4 km point so take appropriate extra footwear. Bicycles are not allowed beyond the ford of Burstall Creek, but make the trail to this point much faster and more enjoyable, particularly on the way down.

SICKLE SLAB

A	North Crack	8	gear
B	The Hornet*	10cR	gear
C	The Scorpion**	10c	gear
D	The Cobra*	10cR	gear (RPs necessary)
E	Dancing with Myself*	10b	
F	Playing with Myself*	10a	
G	Bloody Fingers*	11a	gear

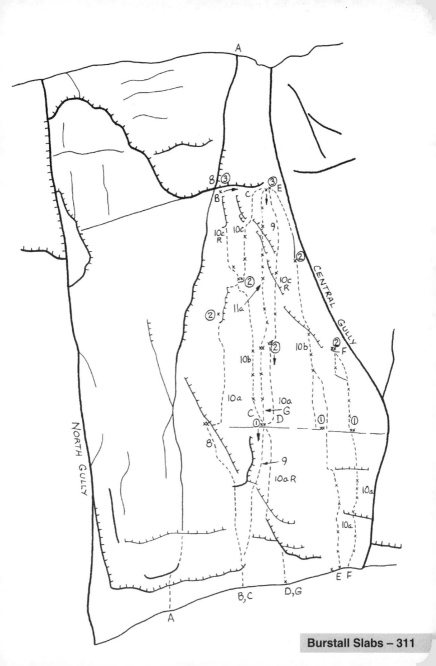

BURSTALL SLABS

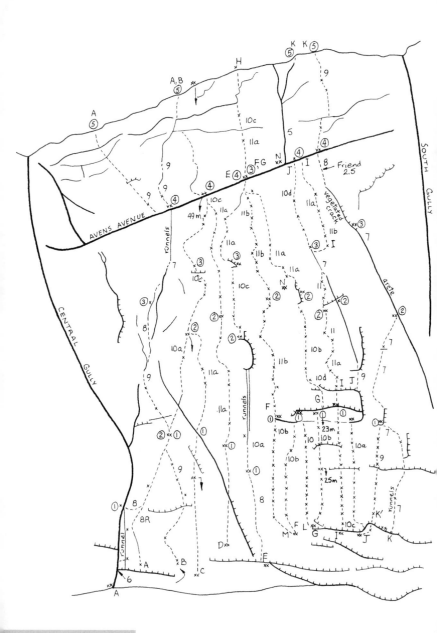

314 – Burstall Slabs

LUNAR SLAB

A	Dark Side of the Moon**	9	gear
B	Moon Shadow**	10c	gear
C	Up the Down Staircase**	11a	gear
D	Space Race**	11a R	gear
E	Moon Dancing**	11a	gear
F	Lunatic Fringe**	11b	
G	Scary Monsters**	11a/b	gear
H	Moon Dancing Continuation*	11a	gear
I	Blue Skies**	11b	gear
J	Apollo**	10d	gear
K	Moonraker**	8 or 9	gear
K'	Moonraker Direct Start**	9	
L	Look Ma, No Hands**	10b	
M	A Touch of Madness**	10b	
N	project		

MOOSE MOUNTAIN (Canyon Creek)

The main appeal of this area is that it can be reached in less than an hour from Calgary and is a sun trap where one can climb on south-facing crags as early as February, if it is sunny and above freezing. Unfortunately, the rock is generally of poor quality because of the intense fracturing that accompanied the formation of the Moose Mountain Dome. The routes described here are on the better patches of rock, are very well protected for leading, and are usually much better than they look. However, they are still quite loose and you should **always wear a helmet!**

Numerous climbers looked at this area through the 1980s and wrote it off as a choss pile, but the late Lawrence Ostrander persisted and set up 70 or so routes that he could work on his own using a shunt. He thought that they would require too much cleaning to set up as regular climbs. Some of Ostrander's routes have now been rebolted for leading and many new ones have been added as well. **Do not attempt to lead routes other than those shown here**—they are Ostrander's old toprope problems and are set up for leading.

Approach

Canyon Creek is located west of the hamlet of Bragg Creek (see map on p. 303). From the 4-way stop sign on the outskirts of Bragg Creek, take Highway 22 south for 3.5 km to the junction with Highway 66. (From south Calgary, this point can be reached via Highway 22X and Priddis.) Turn right (west) and follow Highway 66 for 16 km to Canyon Creek. Cross the bridge and take the next right, opposite the Elbow River boat launch access. Go 600 m to a locked gate across the road and park at the "Ing's Mine Trailhead" on the right. From here it is 4 km (about 15 minutes on a bike) to the bridge at the start of the canyon. There are four major climbing areas, described here in the order in which they are encountered as one travels (west) up Canyon Creek.

Larry's Gym: This is the small light-coloured north-facing crag that sits just above the south (left) side of the road 300 m beyond the bridge. The right side is undercut, providing overhanging starts to the climbs there.

Moose Patch: 50 m to the west of Larry's Gym is a small buttress beside the river which bears a plaque dedicated to the memory of Lawrence Ostrander. 350 m farther along the road there is a green pipeline valve (LBV 3) on the right. The Moose patch is located on the south-facing cliffs above and right of this. Its most distinctive feature is a prominent line of corners (route G) which diagonals up the cliff from left to right and meets the right end of a broad notch in the top of the wall. Routes A - E are located about 20 m left of this line while routes H - M are on a broad stripe of dark grey rock, about 60 m to its right. The access trail starts about 100 m right of the pipeline valve at a small clump of trees on the bench just above the road. This switchbacks up the slope, arriving at the start of *Moose Lips* (2 - 3 minutes from the road).

The Dust Bowl: The Dust Bowl is the sunniest and steepest crag in the valley and was Ostrander's favourite. He had about 50 shunt problems set up here and you will find his old

The Dust Bowl   LG Larry's Groove   O The Ostrander   FM Fecal Matters

anchors, chain link hangers, bits of tat and wire cables all over the crag. It's worth pondering the huge effort that all this must have taken. The cliff is part of the same band of rock as the Moose Patch and can be reached from there by following a rough trail that runs west along the foot of the cliff. However, it is best approached directly from the road. 300 m west of the pipeline valve the trees on the right side of the road thin out, affording a clear view of a section of cliffs endowed with an abundance of large overhangs; this is the Dust Bowl. The access trail starts 50 m farther to the west, just before the road starts to rise gently and curve to the right. Look for a fresh blaze on a poplar tree and follow a game trail directly up the slope to switchbacks cut into the hillside. After a couple of minutes you will arrive at the crag 5 m right of *The Ostrander*.

Morning Side Crag: From the old Ice Caves parking area at the end of the road (6.5 km from Highway 66), cross the main creek and follow the dry bed of the tributary stream ahead up the hill for 10 minutes to a rock wall. Head right, steeply at first, and follow a trail along the base of the cliff for 50 m to the base of the prominent left-facing chimney/flake system of *Sunrise Crack*.

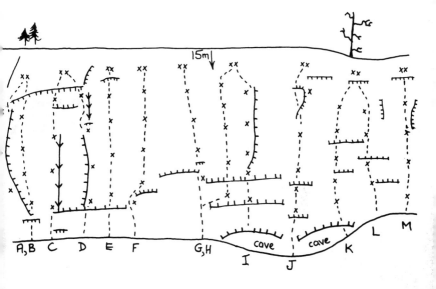

LARRY'S GYM

A Larry's Crack*   9
B Dark Carnival**   10b
C Playing with Shade*   10b
D Fun House**   10a/b
E Dark Secrets**   10d/11a
F Shaddy Delight*   11a
G Pumping Shade*   11b
H Side Show**   11b
I Larry's Gym*   11d
J Larry's Dark Side**   11b
K Larry's Big Picture Show**   11b
L Shadow Man**   11c
M End of the Game*   11a

Dave Carley bouldering at White Buddha.
Photo Sue Slaght.

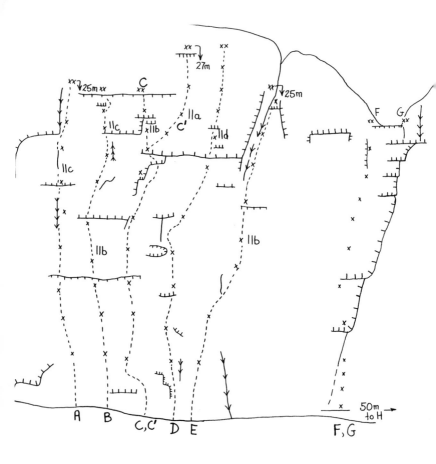

THE MOOSE PATCH, LEFT

A I Fall to Pieces* 11c
B Shattered Logic* 11c
C Spring Clean Up* 11b
C' Spring Clean Out* 11a
D Seasonal Adjustment* 11d
E The Moose Is Loose 11b
F project
G project

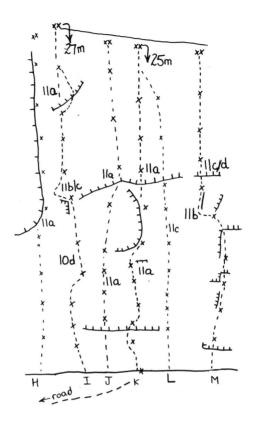

THE MOOSE PATCH, RIGHT

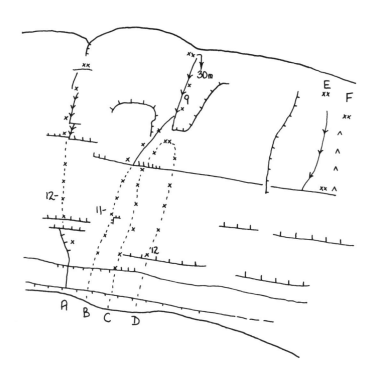

THE DUST BOWL, LEFT

A	Larry's Groove	12a/b
B	Heat Trap	11a/b
C	Fossil Fool	11a
D	Winter Fun	12b/c
E	project	
F	project	

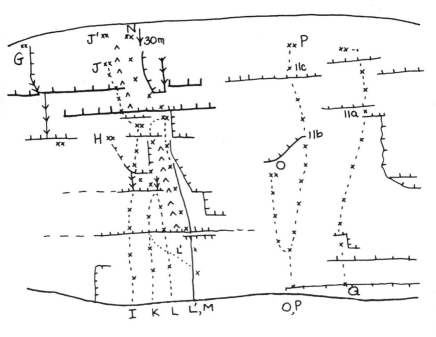

THE DUST BOWL, RIGHT

G	project	
H	project	
I	Donkey Attack	12a
J	Sockdolager	12+
J'	project	
K	Abnormanation	12a
L	Abnormanation, direct start	12+
L'	Abnormanation, alt. start	12a
M	The Ostrander	11b/c
N	project	
O	The House of Pancakes	11c
P	Good 'til the Last Drop	11c
Q	Fecal Matters	11a

Note: Quality rating are not given for these climbs as most have had too few ascents for consensus to be reached.

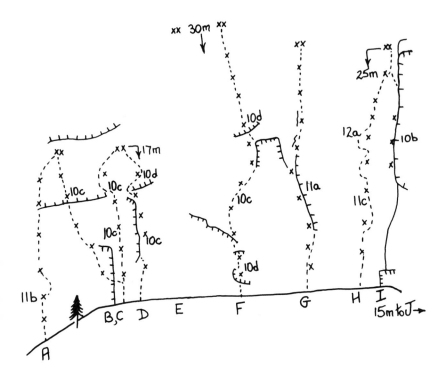

MORNING SIDE CRAG, LEFT

A Wrong Side of the Bed*   11b
B Morning Coffee*   10c
C Breakfast Special*   10c
D Delicious Dessert*   10d
E project
F Special Blend**   11a
G Stones in the Path**   11a
H Wake Up Call**   12a
I Sunrise Crack*   10b   gear to 3.5"

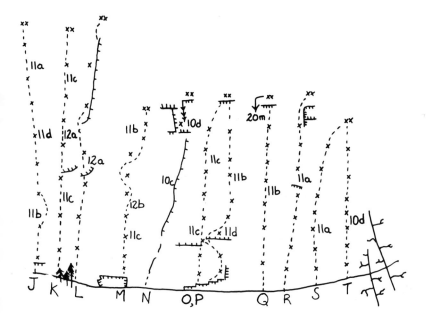

MORNING SIDE CRAG, RIGHT

J	Morning Side**	11d	
K	Morning Stiffy**	12a/b	
L	Dividing Pine**	12a	
M	I'm Gonna Be Strong**	12b	
N	Traditional Moose**	10d	gear to 3.5"
O	Early Riser**	11c	
P	Tiptoe Through the Two Lips*	11d	
Q	Rise and Shine**	11b	
R	Mr Sandman**	11a	
S	Morning Light*	11a	
T	Twin Pines**	10d	

PRAIRIE CREEK

This area is located along Prairie Creek, the next drainage west of Canyon Creek (see map on p. 303). The rock is generally overhanging, sometimes exceedingly so, and is riddled with solution pockets that range in size from shallow monos to both-hands buckets. Where well groomed, the rock is fairly solid, but expect to pop holds if you stray from the usual path. The cliff faces north and thus is best visited in summer, although it seeps after heavy rainfall. The majority of the best climbs here are in the 5.12 - 5.13 range.

Approach
Take Highway 66 to the gate at Elbow Falls, 2.5 km west of Canyon Creek (see p. 316). Park on the left in the Beaver Lodge pull-out, 400 m farther ahead. Cross the road and follow a trail in the ditch back right and down the embankment to Prairie Creek. Continue upstream for approximately 20 minutes to a viewpoint atop a prominent rocky spur. The crag is now visible—a narrow band of rock that slants down the hillside from left to right, just below the skyline on the opposite side of the creek and slightly upstream of here. The trail now descends from the viewpoint to creek level. From the bottom of the hill, continue about another 250 m to a small trail that cuts sharply to the left at a cairn just before the start of a short, steep hill on the main trail (approximately 30 minutes from the parking area). Follow the side trail and cross the creek via logs or three boulders. Turn right, follow a faint trail upstream and then angle up a short, mossy scree slope to the base of the cliff band. The first climbs are located just left of here on a small but steep buttress (The Libido Cafe) beside a staging area. Left of here (in order) are: Le Secteur Bumbly, Petra, The Soft Rock Cafe, Midan Tahrir, Illusion Buttress and The Korova Milk Bar.

THE LIBIDO CAFE

A Whip It*   V7-9 (height dependent)
B Tool and Injection**   V7
C Fat**   12d
D Ace Frehley   11c
E Spro   12c

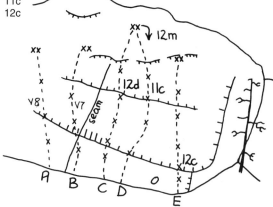

LE SECTEUR BUMBLY

A Out on a Limb   10d
B Bombus**   11a
C Pleb*   9+
D Grimmia*   10b

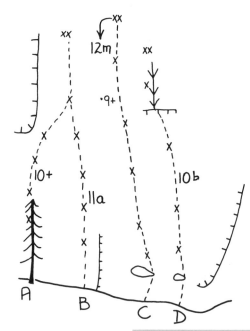

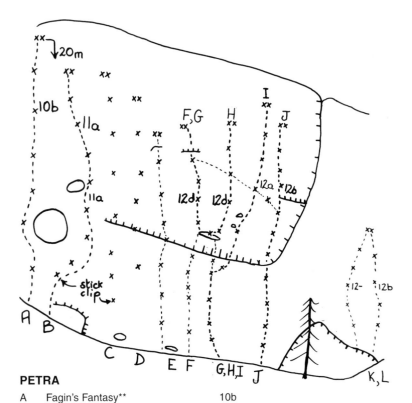

PETRA

A	Fagin's Fantasy**	10b
B	Babe**	11a/b
C	project	
D	project	
E	Deep Shag**	13a
F	A67**	13a
G	Heavy Wetting**	12d
H	Booty Juice**	12d
I	The Mighty Expectation of Relief**	12a
J	This Week in Bible Prophecy**	12b
K	The Blink's Powerful**	11d/12a
L	Slot Jockeys**	12b

Link-ups:

J - I		12b
J - F	Swimming to Cambodia**	13/ab

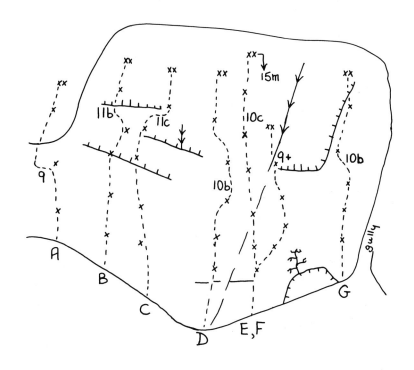

THE SOFT ROCK CAFE

A	Sidestep	9
B	Double Digit Inflation	11b
C	A Pine in the Ass*	11c
D	Scat*	10b
E	Raisin' Sex**	10c
F	Seeing Red*	9/10a
G	Blind Faith**	10b

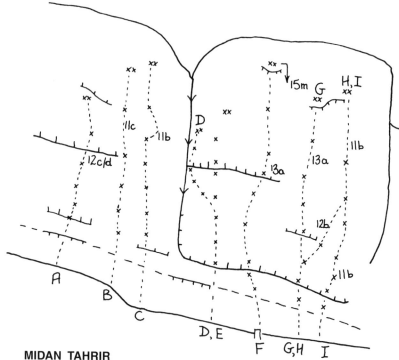

MIDAN TAHRIR

A Hot Pants Explosion*   12c/d
B English Soccer Hooligans*   11c/d
C The Jester*   11b
D Escape Pod   12a
E open project
F Con Dila*   13a
G The Silver Rocket**   13a
H Westland Dodge**   12b
I The Cryocooler**   11b

ILLUSION BUTTRESS

A   Playing the Slots*   11b/c
B   project
C   No Rest for the Wicked**   12a

THE KOROVA MILK BAR

A   Alberta Bound   9+
B   Got Mersey Beat   8+
C   Fuzzy Wobble*   11b/c
D   Roy Batty*   12c
E   Manic*   12d
F   Hermetically Sealed** 12a
G   Moloko Plus**   11a/b
H   Droog*   10b

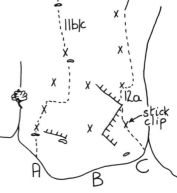

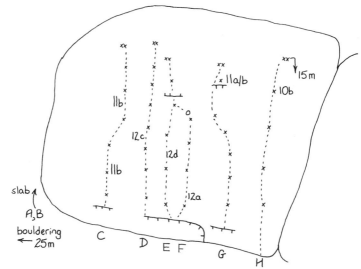

THE WHITE BUDDHA

The White Buddha is located along Powderface Creek, the next drainage south of Prairie Creek (see map p. 303). It is primarily a bouldering area, although there are also a dozen or so short (10 - 12 m) lead climbs. The area is a sun trap and climbing is possible even in winter—*if* it is a few degrees or so above zero, sunny and *calm*. The slope below the crag stays relatively snow-free in winter and any snow on Powderface Trail is usually packed down, so the approach is usually still easy, although sometimes in spring it may be very icy. During winter, the area is usually warmest from late morning to mid-afternoon, before the Chinook winds kick in. Bring plenty of warm clothes—you may be climbing in a T-shirt one minute but, if the wind gets up, freezing your butt off the next. If you use contact lenses bring glasses to wear, as it is *very* dirty around the crag if it is windy.

Approach

Take Highway 66 to the gate at Elbow Falls (closed from December 1 - May 15). Continue west for another 500 m before turning right into the Powderface Creek parking area. Follow the trail from the far left corner of the parking area up and over a hill until you cross Powderface Creek, which is usually dry (about 10 minutes from parking). From here, two prominent bands of light grey rock are visible on the hillside to the right; White Buddha is the upper of these. Continue along the trail for another 2 - 3 minutes until you reach a point where the lower rock band almost meets the trail. (If you reach the remains of an old gate across the trail, you have gone about 150 m too far.) Cut up the bank above and follow a rough trail (flagged) that skirts the left edge of the lower rock band and then zigzags up the open slope above to the crag, joining it at the leftmost lead climbing buttress (Mello Jello), about 10 minutes from the main trail. The main bouldering areas are located just right of here and comprise two sections of undercut, bulging, pocketed limestone in the middle of the crag. Right of these is a slabby face (Weenie Wall) flanked on its right by a steeper face (Gravity Boy).

Note: This is *not* a good area to go bouldering on your own as it is still new and holds may be fragile or wet. Some of the problems are traverses; many go up just a few moves (and then you jump down); a few are set up for toproping—there are 2 sets of Super Shut anchors that can be stick-clipped and directional hangers so that you can work several problems from each anchor. Bring a crash pad for bouldering.

MELLO JELLO (opposite, top)

A	Mello Jello	10a/b
B	Shake and Bake*	10c
C	The Half Pipe**	9
D	Winter Burn*	10c

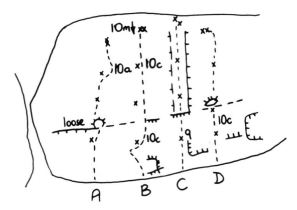

MELLO JELLO (see opposite page)

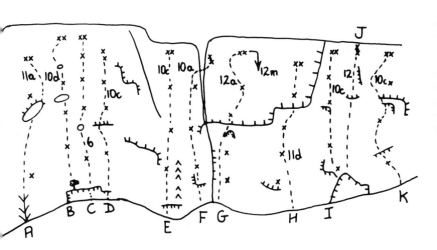

WEENIE WALL

A	Boloney	11a
B	Read My Lips	10d
C	Teenie Weenie**	6
D	Baking Batteries*	10c
E	I Wish It Were Longer**	10c
F	Shake, Rattle and Roll	10a/b

GRAVITY BOY

G	The End is the Beginning*	12a
H	Gravity Boy**	11d
I	Cool Running*	10c
J	Crocodile Shoes*	12a
K	Bananas*	10c

INDEX

344 – Index